ULTRALIGHT AIRMAN'S MANUAL

ULTRALIGHT AIRMAN'S MANUAL

BEN MILLSPAUGH

TAB BOOKS Inc.
Blue Ridge Summit, PA

FIRST EDITION
SECOND PRINTING

Copyright © 1987 by TAB BOOKS Inc.
Printed in the United States of America

Library of Congress Cataloging in Publication Data

Millspaugh, Ben P.
Ultralight airman's manual.

Includes index.
1. Ultralight aircraft.   2. Ultralight aircraft—
Piloting.   I. Title.
TL685.15.M55   1986   629.133′343   86-6022
ISBN 0-8306-2391-4 (pbk.)

TAB BOOKS Inc. offers software for
sale. For information and a catalog,
please contact TAB Software Department,
Blue Ridge Summit, PA 17294-0850.

Questions regarding the content of this book
should be addressed to:

Reader Inquiry Branch
TAB BOOKS Inc.
Blue Ridge Summit, PA 17294-0214

Contents

Acknowledgments

One of the nicest things about being an author is the opportunity to say "thanks" to friends and supporters. It would be impossible for me to give recognition to every student, instructor, weather briefer, and critic that made a positive contribution to this book. However, there are a few who really did help directly, and I would like to say thanks to them.

To instructors Ron Benham and David Ravetti, I want to express my appreciation for their input in the flight section. Both of these fine CFIs made a very positive contribution—not only to this manual, but to the overall betterment of the sport. I want to thank Mr. Fred Bailey, Chief Ground Instructor of the Emery School of Aviation, for his help in proofing the first draft. Fred is a very knowledgeable instructor and he has a way of surfacing errors that I miss.

I also want to thank all of those ground school students who used this book and gave their input for overall improvement and accuracy.

Finally, I would like to thank Mike McQuiddy for making the first publication possible. Mike threw his heart and soul into the sport of ultralight flying and he deserves to be recognized for wanting to upgrade the training of future pilots.

This book is dedicated to my son Frank and my daughter Shawn. They were always there in the cheering section when I needed them most.

ULTRALIGHT AIRMAN'S MANUAL

Introduction

The ultralight aircraft is an airplane in the same sense that a sailboard is a boat. The sailboard floats on the surface of the water and is propelled forward by manipulation of a device that captures the energy of the wind. An ultralight is a device that achieves lift by the dynamic reaction of the relative wind upon the surface of its wings. I could imagine that many traditional sailors will argue this, just as many traditional aviators will argue that an ultralight is not an airplane.

When I first saw an ultralight at the National Aerospace Conference in Orlando, Florida, I was intrigued. I thought to myself, here's an opportunity to get huge numbers of people into General Aviation. The idea of a "chicken in every pot and an airplane in every garage" was fascinating—even possible! During a demonstration to our group, the little craft was launched from an area about the size of a soccer field. This model, made by Hi-Nuski, was a weight-shift craft and just watching the skilled pilot fly around the area was a delight.

In the fall of 1981 I bought a Quicksilver MX and the fun began. During that year, I was called upon to teach ground schools for several ultralight companies, and from that experience I wrote the book *Ultralight Airman's Manual*. This manual is based, for the most part, on the needs of the ultralight fliers I taught in my ground training courses.

That brings me to the next point: Just who flies ultralights? The people who enrolled in my courses ranged from zero-timers to a couple of airline pilot instructors who wanted to see what, if any, difference there was. For the most part, the people I instructed were zero-timers with a strong interest in flying. For them, going the General Aviation route was much too expensive—and in a few cases, out of the question. By the latter, I am referring to the pilot who had lost his medical and still wanted to fly. Most of my ground school students were between the ages of 19 and 40; they arrived in everything from motorcycles to pickup trucks. Once in the classroom, they all shared the fellowship of flying. They looked and sounded like any gathering of aviators. They deserved a good course and I did my best to give them quality instruction.

The ground school courses were based on a curriculum that was similar to that given pilot trainees everywhere. However, the ultralight aircraft is, by law, "tethered" to a 40 mile radius, and my training concentrated on local flying situations. I taught aerodynamics, weather, local navigation, local law, and the basics of flight control. With the exception of three or four, all of my students went from ground school to flight training.

A book is limited in what it can impart to some- one in training. The real knowledge of flight can only come from one source—experience. Use this book as a resource in your ground/flight training and constantly update your knowledge with other publications. Like all aviators, past and present, you must constantly study to become more proficient. It is the intent of this book to acquaint you with some of the basics necessary to help you along the path to proficiency.

Chapter 1

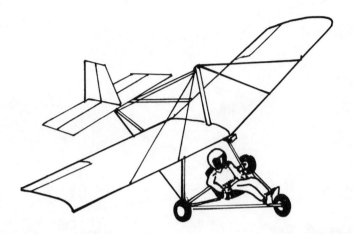

The Ultralight Aircraft

Before undertaking a study of any technical subject, it's important for the student to have a thorough knowledge of the language of components. This is especially true with aircraft, since your background in the automobile will not transfer. Airplanes are totally different and about the only similarity is in the wheels and tires! Therefore, take a moment to look over the components of the ultralight and the two-stroke powerplant.

AIRCRAFT COMPONENTS

Figure 1-1 shows a modified (clipped wing) Quicksilver MX that was produced in 1982. This aircraft was a very popular ultralight and was considered an industry leader in its time. Figure 1-2 shows components of a typical three-axis ultralight. Figure 1-3 shows a light General Aviation aircraft similar to a Cessna 152. Now take some time and compare the components of all three and you will better understand the nomenclature that will be referred to in the balance of the text.

The Quicksilver MX shown in Fig. 1-1 is not a three-axis ultralight in the traditional sense. Notice the component about midway between the front and rear of the wing closest to you. This is actually a spoiler that acts somewhat like the ailerons shown in Fig. 1-2. More about the operation of these and other control devices follows.

THE ULTRALIGHT ENGINE

The ultralight engine is basically a simple powerplant that is easy to maintain and very reliable. From the very beginning, ultralights have been powered by two-stroke engines that were lightweight and powerful for their size. Snowmobile engines were a natural, since they were relatively inexpensive and had available modifications for operation at high altitudes.

A typical two-stroke ultralight engine is shown in Fig. 1-4. This is one of the earlier Cuyuna powerplants found on the popular Quicksilver aircraft. Other companies have been equally popular and the technology has produced very high quality, high-power, efficient engines.

Fig. 1-1. Quicksilver MX ultralight aircraft.

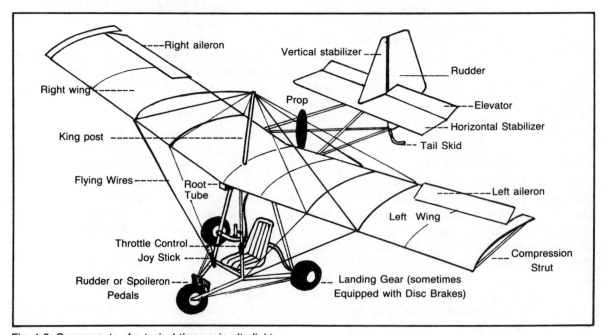

Fig. 1-2. Components of a typical three-axis ultralight.

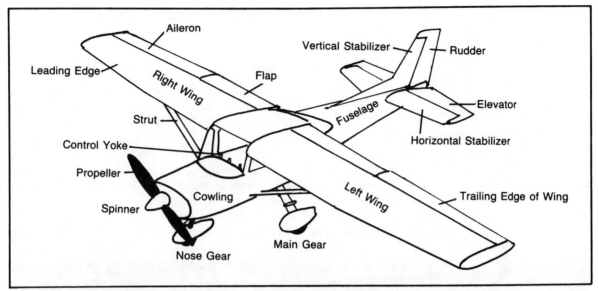

Fig. 1-3. General aviation training aircraft.

Fig. 1-4. Fuel system components of two-stroke ultralight aircraft engine.

Figures 1-4, 1-5 and 1-6 show the various components of the Cuyuna engine; for the most part, all two-stroke ultralight engines are similar. Like the aircraft nomenclature, it is a good idea to review the components before further study.

TWO-STROKE THEORY OF OPERATION

While on the subject of engines, now is a good time to go over the basic theory behind the two-stroke. The good people at Cuyuna Engine Company have given their permission to reprint an excellent operation pamphlet called "Two Stroke Theory of Operation." With sincere thanks from your author and TAB Books, Inc., here is the story

behind the device that makes the propeller do its job:

Intake

The first step in an engine's work cycle is the *intake* of fuel and air from the carburetor. In order to get the mixture into the crankcase area, there must be an opening (port) along with some kind of valve to open and close the port. In most two-cycle engines, the piston acts as the valve. When the piston begins to move up in the cylinder, the movement creates a partial vacuum or low-pressure area in the crankcase. As the piston continues to ascend, the piston skirt uncovers a hole in the cylinder, the

Fig. 1-5. The ignition system of ultralight engine.

Fig. 1-6. Right side of the Cuyuna engine showing exhaust system.

intake port (Fig. 1-7). Since the mixture flows from a high pressure area to a low pressure area, the crankcase and lower portion of the cylinder are filled with a fresh fuel mixture. This fresh mixture remains in the engine and completely fills the crankcase and lower cylinder. The mixture is used to lubricate the crankshaft main and needle bearings until the piston starts to descend and uncovers the transfer ports.

Transfer

The second step is the *transfer* of the fresh fuel mixture in the crankcase to the cylinder. As the piston begins the downward stroke, the fuel mixture in the crankcase is compressed. When the piston slides past the transfer ports (Fig. 1-8), the fuel mix-

ture is forced to the lower pressure area of the cylinder bore. This continues until the ports are completely uncovered and the piston is at bottom dead center (BDC).

The basic transfer port design has two important functions. The transfer port must move the mixture from the crankcase to the cylinder. Also, the transfer port must help the engine get rid of (scavenge) exhaust gases from the cylinder. Before the transfer port can operate correctly, the exhaust gases rush out of the cylinder until the internal engine pressure equals external pressure (ambient pressure). At this point the exhaust gases will quit flowing. The transfer ports must aim the incoming fresh mixture in such a way to aid the removal of any remaining burned gases.

5

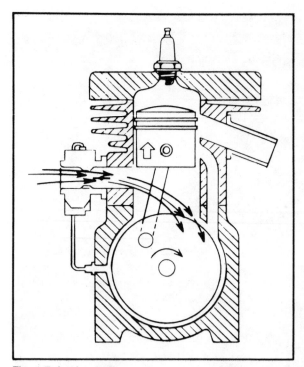

Fig. 1-7. Intake stroke.

point before top dead center (BTDC), an electrical spark jumps the air gap between the center and side electrode of the spark plug. This causes the compressed combustible mixture to ignite (burn). At normal cranking speeds, the spark occurs at slightly before top dead center (BTDC); however, the spark advances fully as the engine speed increases. The spark can be advanced by either mechanical or electrical means, depending on the ignition system used (Fig. 1-9).

Even though the combustion phase is nearly identical to that of a four-stroke engine, and can suffer from the same abnormalities (detonation, pre-ignition, etc.), the two-stroke engine's power stroke is shorter than that of a four-stroke engine. Because more exhaust gases remain in the fresh mixture in a two-stroke engine, the combustion temperature is also lower. Also, for this reason, the output of

The shape and size of the transfer ports are also critical to proper engine scavenging. If a port is too large, the fuel flow will drop and the lack of inertia will affect the flow pattern after the mixture leaves the port. Too small a port will restrict the flow of the incoming mixture. By controlling the angle of the transfer ports, ports can be enlarged to great degree and still be effective at low engine speeds. Also, since the transfer port is part of the crankcase area, removal of existing metal will decrease the pressure of the crankcase area while at the same time increasing the volume to be filled.

Compression and Ignition

The third step in a two-cycle engine is *compression*. Compression occurs only after all the ports in the upper part of the cylinder are closed. At this point, the mixture is compressed by the upward motion of the piston from bottom dead center (BDC). As the piston reaches a specific predetermined

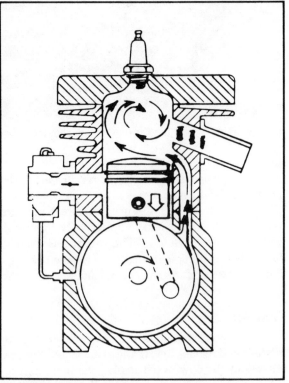

Fig. 1-8. Transfer of fuel/air charge to the combustion chamber.

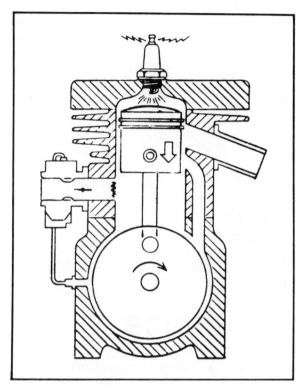

Fig. 1-9. Compression and ignition.

nitrogen oxides is reduced by the quantity of un-burned hydrocarbons is increased. The oil used in the two-stroke engine is also greater than in a four-stroke engine and results in more unburned hydrocarbons.

Expansion (Power)

The *power* stroke begins just after the igniting of the fuel mixture. The burning gases expand and force the piston downward by exerting the maximum combustion pressure on the piston dome. The downward force is then transmitted through the crankshaft connecting rod and, because of the crankshaft design, is converted to radial motion. In a two-stroke engine the power stroke is completed when the piston begins to clear the exhaust port opening.

Even though the two-stroke engine has a shorter power pulse, it occurs twice as often as in a four-stroke engine. This enables a two-stroke engine to achieve a high specific output when compared to the output of an identical size four-stroke engine. Thus, two identical displacement engines (one two-stroke and one four-stroke) will produce different performance readings. The two-stroke engine will produce a specific horsepower at a lower engine speed than an identical displacement four-stroke engine. This is the reason nearly all two-stroke engines have a higher horsepower/displacement ratio for any specific engine speed than the same displacement four-stroke engine.

Exhaust

The final step of the engine work cycle is the *exhaust* of burned combustion gases from the cylinder through the exhaust port. When the piston slides by the exhaust port (Fig. 1-10), most of the exhaust gases are expelled; however, some remain in the cylinder. As the piston slides by the transfer ports,the incoming mixture forces the remaining gases out of the cylinder.

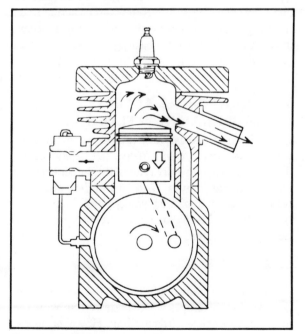

Fig. 1-10. Exhaust.

Chapter 2

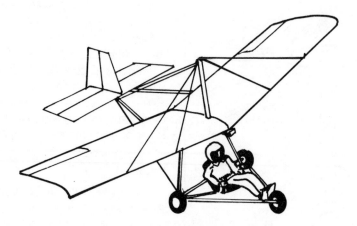

Basic Aerodynamics

The ultralight aircraft is like any other airplane in one very special way: It has four forces acting upon it in flight and it is necessary that you learn them at this point. Two of these forces are artificial and two are natural (Fig. 2-1).

THE FOUR FORCES ACTING ON AN ULTRALIGHT IN FLIGHT

Lift, drag, thrust, and gravity are the four forces and two, *lift* and *thrust*, are produced by devices that dynamically react with the air through which the craft moves. *Gravity* and *drag* are natural forces and will be with you always. There is another force which balances the aircraft and it will be discussed later.

LIFT

For years, man sought to find the secret of flying. At first, attempts were made to flap wings in an effort to emulate birds in flight. However, it was not until some serious scientific breakthroughs oc-

curred that man had the technology to create a flying machine.

An enormous scientific event occurred when a Swiss scientist by the name of Daniel Bernoulli observed the changes in fluid motion with a device called the venturi (Fig. 2-2). Bernoulli found that as a fluid, such as air, passed through the venturi's restricted middle, the pressure would drop and the velocity would increase. This inverse proportion is the "secret" to the aerodynamic reaction a wing has with the airflow around it. It truly is the secret of lift and flight.

The Airfoil

Let's face it—without a wing, you're not a flying machine. Look at the official FAA definition of an airplane: " . . . is supported in flight by the dynamic reaction of the air against its wing." The big question is, how does it work? To better understand lift and how it's produced, we have to go back to the work of the Swiss scientist, Daniel Bernoulli. Bernoulli found that the *pressure* of a fluid, such

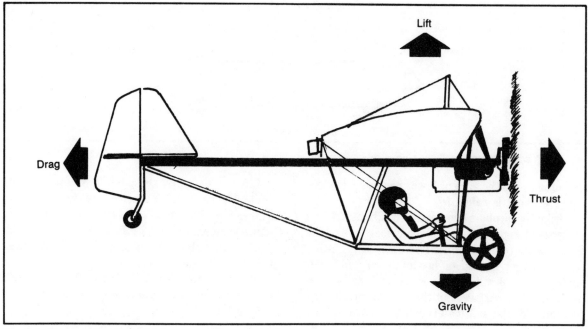

Fig. 2-1. The four forces in flight.

as a liquid or a gas, decreases at points where the *speed* of the fluid increases. The most notable use of this law is in the creation of lift. The shape of the wing causes the air passing over the upper surface to go faster than the air passing under the wing. Using the Bernoullian law, you can see that this increase in speed causes the pressure to decrease. Because the pressure (relatively speaking) on the bottom of the wing is higher, the entire airfoil moves into the area of lower pressure. This

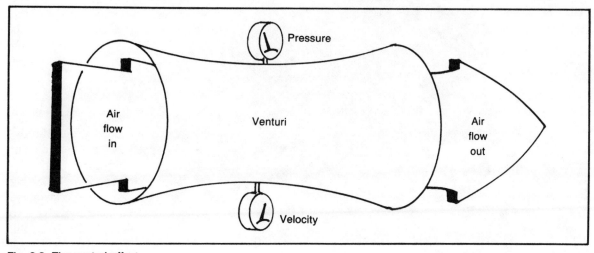

Fig. 2-2. The venturi effect.

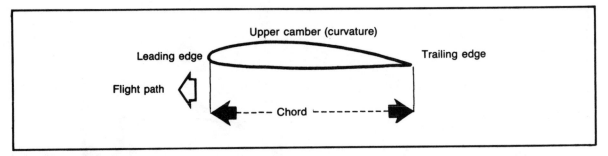

Fig. 2-3. A conventional airfoil showing component parts.

movement into the area of lower pressure, if it opposes gravity, is called *lift*.

Like the airplane comparison in Chapter 1, the wing also has parts. Let's take a closer look at the components of a conventional airfoil. (Fig. 2-3).

A conventional airfoil has an upper and lower surface. The ultralight, in some cases, has an upper and lower surface, but they are basically, the two sides of the sail material (Fig. 2-4).

Lift is created by the passage of air over the airfoil because of the decreased pressure above its surface. Simultaneously, the impact of air on the underside increases the pressure below. It has been estimated that about 70 percent of the lift is created on the upper side of the airfoil.

There are four ways of increasing lift in flight. The ultralight utilizes the first two of these. They are:

Fig. 2-4. Side view of Rotec airfoil.

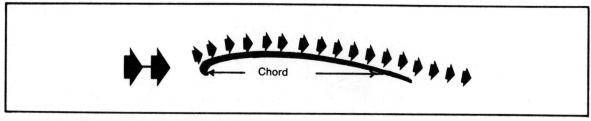

Fig. 2-5. Ultralight airfoil showing relative wind (black arrows).

☐ Increase lift by increasing speed.
☐ Increase lift by an increase in angle of attack.
☐ Increase lift by increasing camber (flaps, slats, etc.).
☐ Increase lift by increasing wing area (Fowler Flap).

It isn't too difficult to see how lift could be increased by an increase in speed. This simply means more air over the wing gives a greater pressure differential and the wing lifts more.

Relative Wind and Angle of Attack

All right, let's take a close look at the airfoil as we increase the wing's angle of attack. Note Fig. 2-5. We have a conventional ultralight wing, flying straight and level. The black arrow shows the relative wind, opposite in direction to the flight path. In Fig. 2-6, the relative wind would look like this in a climb. In Fig. 2-7, the wing looks like it's climbing, but it's not. This is a high angle of attack. The angle between the chord line and the relative wind is the *angle of attack*.

The relative wind is produced by the forward

motion of the airplane. Remember, during actual flight, the forward movement, or speed, is your life. You need forward velocity to fly. The speed and direction of surface wind has little effect on the *relative wind*. Look at relative wind this way: imagine a child playing next to a bathtub with a toy boat on a string. Now, the water in the bathtub isn't going anywhere, so we could assume it is standing still. When the child pulls on the string, the boat moves. The water, relative to the boat is moving backward. The same would apply to the airplane. Even in still air, when power is applied and the propeller thrusts the craft forward, the relative wind starts to move opposite to the direction of the flight. Lift acts perpendicular to the relative wind, and to the wing span. (*Span* is distance from tip to tip.) In Fig. 2-8, we see a 10 degree angle of attack even in a climb. This would be an example of a takeoff where you need the greater lift to climb away from the airport.

In Fig. 2-9 we have a descent and a 10 degree angle of attack is increased to slow the aircraft down, due to greater drag, and to allow a slower airspeed for landing. The wing is still lifting although it is flying slower, a good setup for an ap-

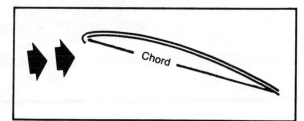

Fig. 2-6. Ultralight airfoil in steep climb. The relative wind is down and backward.

Fig. 2-7. Ultralight airfoil in a high angle of attack.

11

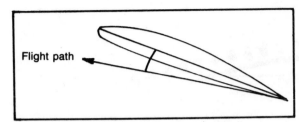

Fig. 2-8. Ten degree angle of attack in a climb.

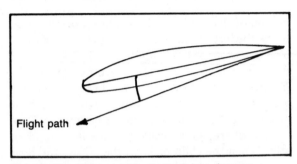

Fig. 2-9. Ten degree angle of attack in a descent.

proach. Again, you must be careful to keep up the flying speed. Let's take a look at the airfoil when it stops flying.

There is a point where the airfoil will no longer provide the additional lift in a high angle of attack. This point is called the *critical angle of attack*. When you exceed the critical angle of attack, the wing will *stall* (Fig. 2-10). Don't get all upset when you hear the word stall; it's generally quite docile in an ultralight. It is simply the point where the wing quits flying and starts to mush and descend. The

only thing you have to watch for is enough altitude to recover.

STALLS

I'm assuming you are aware of the *center of gravity*. You can thank your local aircraft designer for the fact that the center of gravity, in an ultralight, is ahead of the point of maximum lift, or *center of lift*. Why? When the wing stops lifting, the nose will drop—and that is the natural recovery for a stall.

If the critical angle of attack is exceeded, any wing will stall. Don't let some high-pressure ultralight salesperson tell you his bird won't stall; it's just not true!

What about the *canard* setup? In straight and level flight, the canard, out front, will keep the wing from stalling this way. Note in Fig. 2-11, that the canard, a small wing out in front of this ultralight, has a higher *angle of incidence* than the wing. The canard, because of this higher angle of incidence, will also stall first in a high angle of attack, or whenever the critical angle of attack of the canard has been exceeded (Fig. 2-12).

The *angle of incidence* is the *built-in* angle of such things as airfoils, elevators, canards, etc.

The canard, upon reaching its critical angle of attack, will stall first, and because this is a weight-bearing airfoil, will lower the nose of the aircraft, keeping the main wing from reaching its critical angle of attack. When some high-rolling salesman tells

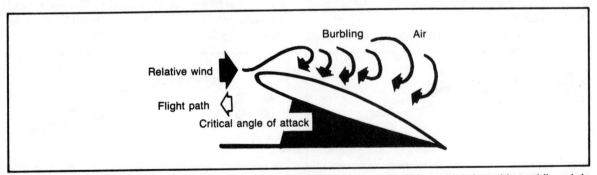

Fig. 2-10. Once the critical angle of attack is exceeded, the relative wind separates and lift is lost; this tumbling air is called burble.

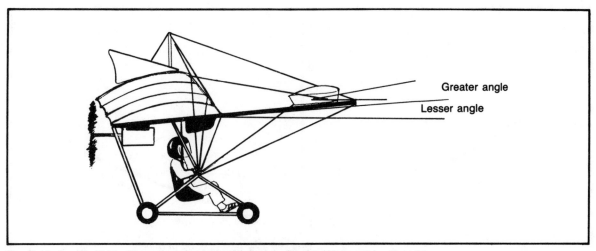

Fig. 2-11. An ultralight with a canard set at a higher angle of incidence than the wing.

you "This canard-equipped airplane will not stall; it's impossible!", don't believe it. *Any wing will stall at any airspeed and in any attitude if the critical angle of attack is exceeded!* Take this for an example: You're flying along and a huge updraft hits the bottom of the canard, pointing you straight up. All of a sudden, your speed nears zero! The airplane is stalled, let there be no doubt in your mind. The nose will (after you've passed over, through, or around

the updraft) pitch forward and once you have some flying speed, the craft will porpoise back into equilibrium. Just hope this event never occurs too close to the ground.

THE THREE AXES

Earlier I talked about the aircraft "nosing" over when a stall occurs. The actual term for nosing over is called *pitch. Pitch, roll,* and *yaw* are terms relat-

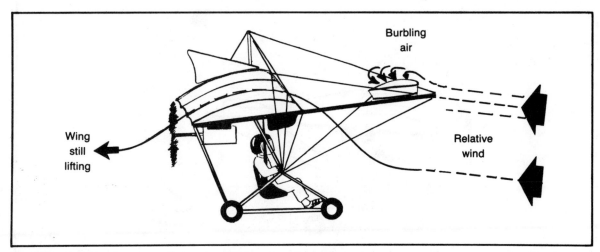

Fig. 2-12. In flight, when the critical angle of attack of the canard has been reached, the canard will stall before the wing stalls. The nose will drop.

13

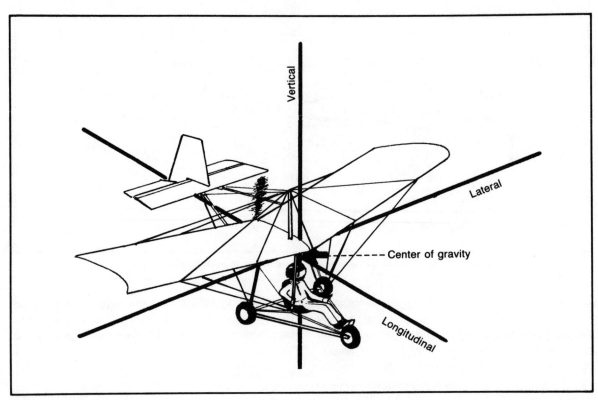

Fig. 2-13. The three axes.

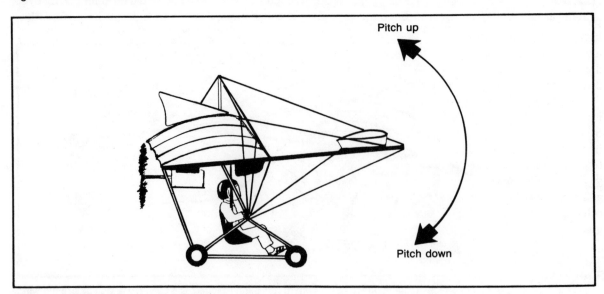

Fig. 2-14. Rotation around the lateral axis.

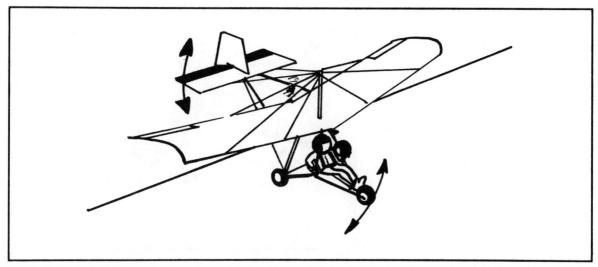

Fig. 2-15. When the elevator is moved up or down, the nose pitches up or down by rotating around the lateral axis.

ing to movements around the airplane's three axes. These axes are *longitudinal, vertical,* and *lateral.*

In Fig. 2-13, you will first see the longitudinal axis. This axis goes through the aircraft from front to rear. Movement around this axis is known as *roll.* The axis that goes through the craft from wingtip to wingtip is called the lateral and movement around this axis is called *pitch.* Finally, the axis that passes through the aircraft from top to bottom is known as the vertical, and movement around this axis is called *yaw.* All of the three axes pass through a point called the *center of gravity.* The terms roll, pitch, and yaw are nautical in derivation.

In a conventional aircraft setup (i.e., the tail being in the rear), we know that certain movements of its control surfaces will cause the aircraft to move in certain directions. The elevator causes the nose to pitch up or down; the rudder causes the nose to yaw right or left; and if the aircraft is equipped with ailerons, movement of these control surfaces will roll the aircraft to the right or left, around the longitudinal axis (Figs. 2-14 through 2-18).

Rudder

In aircraft with conventional three-axis control,

Fig. 2-16. When the rudder moves right or left, the nose moves to the right or left by rotating around the vertical axis. This movement is called yaw.

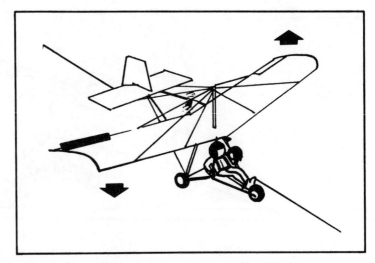

Fig. 2-17. Aileron roll.

including ailerons, the *real* purpose of the rudder, in flight, is to counteract a phenomenon known as *adverse yaw*. Adverse yaw happens this way: When you initiate a roll, or banked turn, the high wing will create more lift than the lower opposite wing. This increase in lift also increases drag. At first, when the roll is initiated, the nose will tend to yaw toward the high wing. This yawing motion is known as *adverse yaw* (Figs. 2-19 through 2-22).

Ruddervators

The *ruddervator* system found on some ultralights is a compromise between the elevator and the rudder. The advantage is that it eliminates one complete control surface and the subsequent drag of that surface (Fig. 2-23).

Elevator and Stabilator

The *elevator* is the control surface that provides a pitch motion around the lateral axis. The elevator is usually hinged to the horizontal stabilizer and is moved up and down by moving the control fore and aft. The flow of air striking the deflected elevator surfaces exerts an upward force, and this in turn causes the elevator surfaces to move downward, or vice versa. The movement pitches the nose up or down (Fig. 2-24).

Essentially, the elevators are controllers of the angle of attack.

Some aircraft have what is known as a *stabilator*. This is a combination of both stabilizer and elevator. When the control stick is moved, the complete stabilator moves and this movement raises or lowers the leading edge. This changes the angle of attack on the stabilator and moves the tail up or down, again rotating the aircraft around the lateral axis (Figs. 2-25 through 2-27).

Another very important control surface is the *canard*. The canard is a front-mounted device that

Fig. 2-18. Roll with spoilerons.

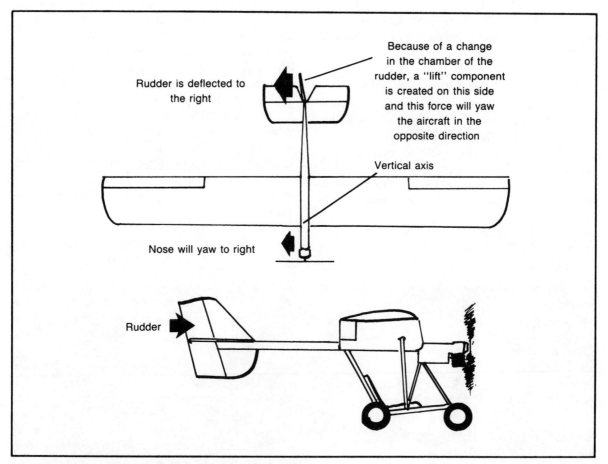

Fig. 2-19. Rudder control system on a Cloudbuster ultralight.

actually carries part of the weight of the aircraft. In other words, it is a "wing." The canard, however, is mounted so that its angle of incidence (the attached angle) is slightly higher than the angle of incidence of the main airfoil, or wing. The canard can be moved so that it pitches the nose of the aircraft up or down. When the aircraft is in a high angle of attack, the canard will stall before the main wing, thus keeping the wing from stalling. However, one must remember that an airfoil can be stalled at any airspeed and in any attitude if the critical angle of attack is exceeded. Under normal circumstances, the canard functions very well keeping the aircraft from developing a full stall.

Ailerons and Spoilerons

To roll the aircraft around the longitudinal axis, the pilot will, if the ultralight is so equipped, deflect the *ailerons*. Some ultralights are equipped with *spoilerons*, which operate by spoiling the lift on one wing, therefore causing a rise on the opposite wing. This drop on one wing and consequent rise on the other rolls the aircraft (Figs. 2-28 through 2-34).

When the spoileron is deflected, a loss of lift occurs on that wing. If both spoilerons are deflected at the same time, the aircraft will sink without gaining speed. This can be an advantage when making an approach to land when you have to come in

17

steep, such as landing over powerlines and trees. You would be losing altitude without picking up airspeed.

Stability around the Three Axes—Lateral

In Fig. 2-35 we see the ultralight in straight and level flight. The aircraft is balanced somewhat like a "teeter-totter." The airplane, in steady state flight (i.e., level unaccelerated flight as well as steady climbs, descents, and turns) has forces that are in equilibrium. You can see in the top illustration the center of lift (large black arrow) is behind the center of gravity. The *tail-down force* maintains a balance along the centerline. Now, when lift decreases, the nose must go down.

This built-in stability factor is a true "confidence-builder" when you think the bird is going to fall right out of the sky if the lift is lost. The wonderful thing about it is when the nose goes down, the aircraft speeds up, relative wind increases over the airfoil, and you are flying again. The arrows illustrated are forces (or, in two of the instances, weights), and the distance from the fulcrum, times the weight, is known as a *moment*. You can easily see how if the center of gravity is very close to the center of lift, a slight shift in CG will nose the aircraft up or down. It all goes back to the days when you were in high school science. Weight times distance from the fulcrum equals a moment. In Fig. 2-36 it would be:

$$W_1 \times D_1 = W_2 \times D_2$$

Fig. 2-20. The control surfaces on the Robertson B1-RD aircraft. The rudder is hinged to a vertical stabilizer.

Fig. 2-21. The rudder on a two-place Quicksilver MX also acts as the vertical stabilizer when aligned to the relative wind.

W_1 would be the weight at the center of gravity and W_2 would be the tail-down force. The D_1 would be the distance from the center of gravity to line connected to the black arrow at the center of lift. D_2 would be the line from the tail-down force to the center of lift.

Let's take a look at the same principle applied to the longitudinal axis. A slight change in the center of gravity, laterally, will cause the aircraft to roll (Fig. 2-37).

Now look at this "CG shift" control system in view of previous diagrams. Any time the center of gravity is very close to the center of lift, a change in the CG will cause a movement around one of the three axes.

In Fig. 2-38, the pilot pushes right or left on the down tubes and the entire center of gravity shifts sideways. This movement translates into a force that causes a rotation around the longitudinal axis, and the aircraft rolls. A shift of the CG in the opposite direction will cancel this roll and bring the aircraft back to straight and level flight. Very often the seat is connected to the rudder and when roll is initiated, so is yaw. This is called *con-*

Fig. 2-22. The wing-mounted rudder of the American Eagle ultralight.

19

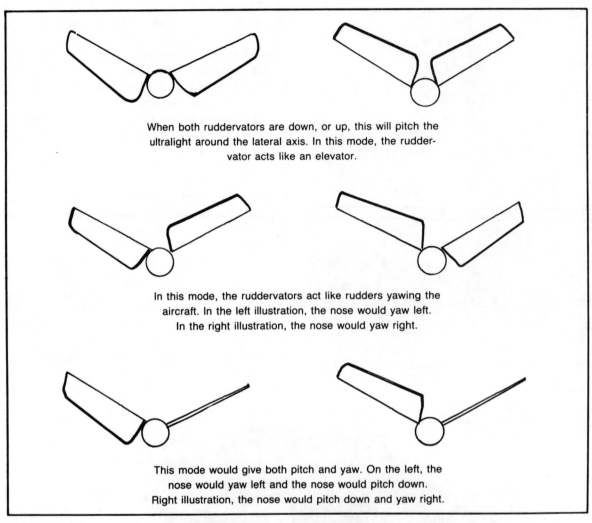

When both ruddervators are down, or up, this will pitch the ultralight around the lateral axis. In this mode, the ruddervator acts like an elevator.

In this mode, the ruddervators act like rudders yawing the aircraft. In the left illustration, the nose would yaw left. In the right illustration, the nose would yaw right.

This mode would give both pitch and yaw. On the left, the nose would yaw left and the nose would pitch down. Right illustration, the nose would pitch down and yaw right.

Fig. 2-23. Ruddervator system. By elimination of the fin, drag is reduced.

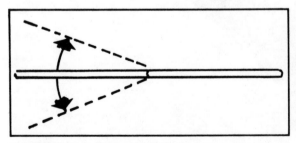

Fig. 2-24. The conventional elevator hinged to a horizontal stabilizer.

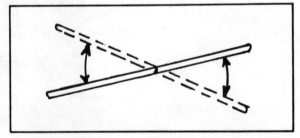

Fig. 2-25. A stabilator is a combined elevator and stabilizer. It is hinged at a central point.

Fig. 2-26. The elevator of the Quicksilver MX.

Fig. 2-27. The control stick of the Rally aircraft.

trol coupling. In Fig. 2-39, the pilot pushes forward on the crossbar, and the CG is shifted rearward, causing the aircraft to pitch its nose upward. By pulling himself forward, the pilot can move the CG forward and this shift will cause the nose of the aircraft to pitch downward (Figs. 2-40, 2-41).

Stability around the Three Axes—Longitudinal

Let's take a look at the lift forces in a turn and I'll show you how the aircraft has a tendency to return to straight and level flight, even though a roll has been initiated.

In Fig. 2-42 you can see that in a turn, the force of lift is divided between the counteraction of weight and centrifugal force. If some correction is not made to keep the aircraft lifting, such as an increase in angle of attack or an increase in thrust, the aircraft will begin a slight descent. Remember, *lift acts perpendicular to the relative wind and to the wing span.*

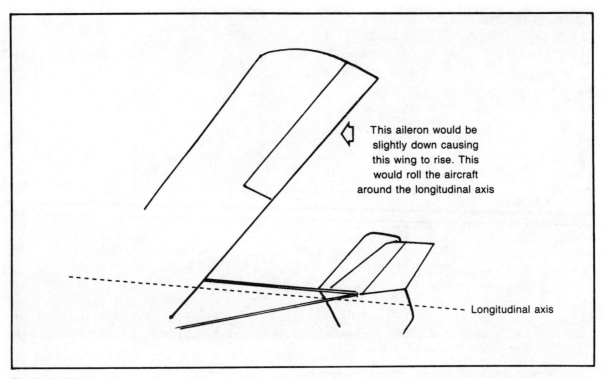

This aileron would be slightly down causing this wing to rise. This would roll the aircraft around the longitudinal axis

Longitudinal axis

Fig. 2-28. Ailerons.

Manufacturers often incorporate what is known as *dihedral* into their aircraft to give stability around the "roll" axis. This is how it works: The low wing is generating more lift than the high wing; there-fore, it has a tendency to right the airplane, bringing it back to straight and level. The greater the dihedral, the more stable the craft is along the roll axis (Fig. 2-43).

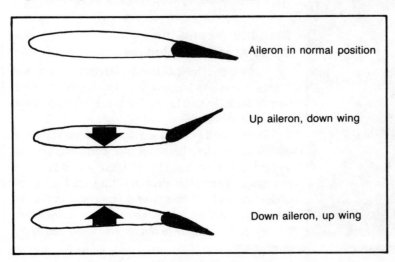

Aileron in normal position

Up aileron, down wing

Down aileron, up wing

Fig. 2-29. Aileron operation.

Fig. 2-30. The aileron of a Robertson B1-RD aircraft.

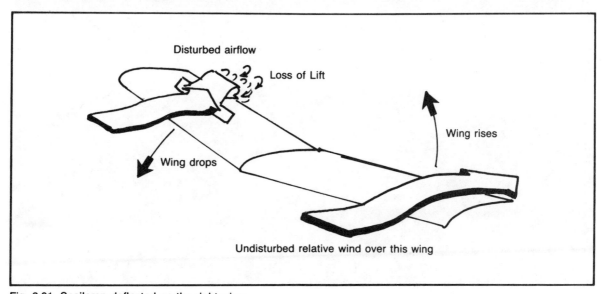

Fig. 2-31. Spoileron deflected on the right wing.

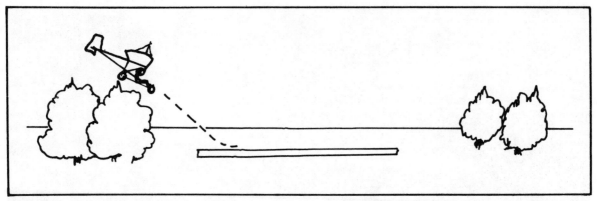

Fig. 2-32. Steep approach using the spoilerons.

Stability Around the Three Axes—Vertical

It is a fact that any airplane, in a conventional configuration, can be turned without banking. This is, of course, done with the rudder. If you yaw the plane to the left, then the left wing will move rearward and the right wing will move forward. Due to the yawing motion, the speed of the relative wind will increase on the right wing and decrease on the left wing. The result is a rolling movement to the left, due to an increase in lift on the right wing and a decrease in lift on the left wing. For this reason, many ultralights aren't equipped with ailerons—and, for that matter, don't really need them.

Many of the canard-type ultralights have wing

Fig. 2-33. Spoilerons on a Rotec Rally aircraft.

Fig. 2-34. Rudder pedals attached to wing mounted spoilerons on a Quicksilver MX.

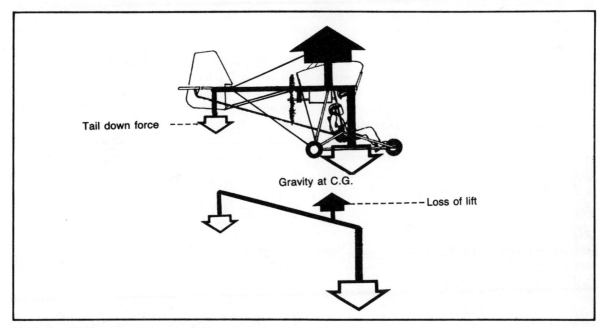

Tail down force

Gravity at C.G.

Loss of lift

Fig. 2-35. Stability around the lateral axis.

25

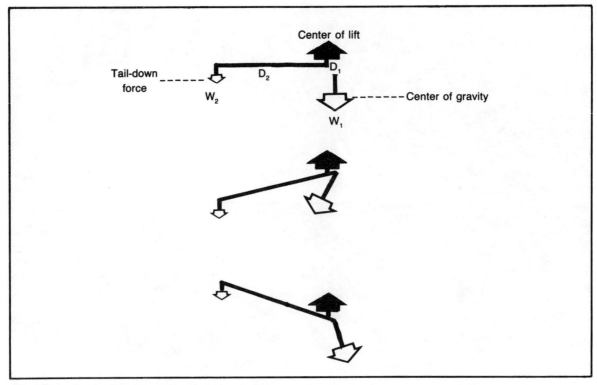

Fig. 2-36. Center of gravity changes causing pitch movements.

rudders that use the above principle for roll control. The yawing motion is very effective for roll at slow speeds and is considered a desirable set up when coupled with a canard.

In Fig. 2-44, we find a "weathervaning" or "slipstream" effect tending to keep the aircraft in equilibrium around the vertical axis. As the aircraft moves, a flow of air moves rearward, providing directional stability. In an ultralight, the fin/rudder is the *primary* source of directional stability.

Load Factor

If you will refer back to Fig. 2-42, you'll see the illustration of centrifugal force. This force actually adds to the weight of the aircraft. Use this example to help understand: Imagine that you put a set of bathroom scales under your fanny in the ultralight during flight, so that you could see the

readout. In a constant 60 degree banked turn, the scales would show your weight *doubled*. You would be pulling 2 Gs.

If *your* weight is doubled, then so must be the weight on the wings of your aircraft. This is called the *load factor*.

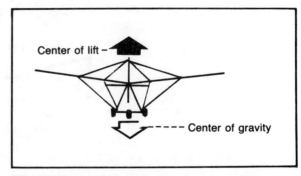

Fig. 2-37. The ultralight flying toward you. Lift balances the weight and the aircraft is stable along the longitudinal axis.

Fig. 2-38. Roll by lateral CG shifting in a variable CG, or weight shift-controlled aircraft.

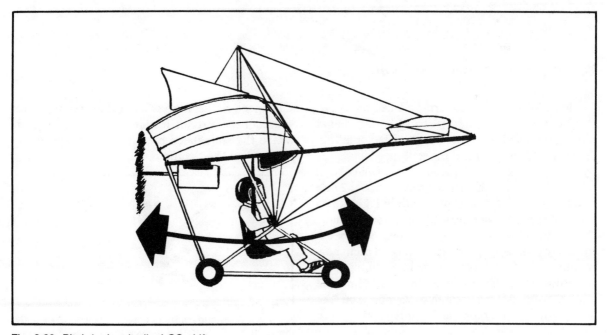

Fig. 2-39. Pitch by longitudinal CG shift.

Fig. 2-40. Variable CG Hi-Nuski Husky ultralight aircraft.

In a 30 degree banked turn, balanced and level, the lift that's necessary to bank a 300 pound ultralight is 346 pounds, and the load factor is 1.15 Gs. It should be noted that the stall speed increases by the square root of the load factor. Going back to our 60 degree bank turn, the square root of 2 (the number of Gs) is 1.414. Now, multiply 1.414 times the stall speed of your ultralight and you will have the number of the stall speed at 60 degree of bank. Let's say your stall speed is normally 20 mph; now multiply 20 times 1.414 and you get 28 mph!

How would this affect you in flight? Imagine you are cruising along leisurely at 25 mph. You spot something on the ground and you bank sharply to take a closer look. Your airspeed falls off and the stall speed rises. If the bank is steep enough, you will stall the aircraft in this situation. The point where the stall speed hits the aircraft speed has been called the "coffin corner."

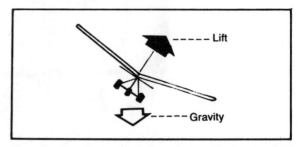

Fig. 2-41. When the center of gravity is shifted to the side, the aircraft will roll in that direction.

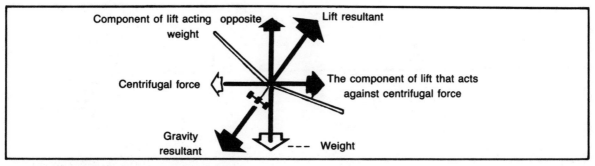

Fig. 2-42. Forces in a turn at a constant bank.

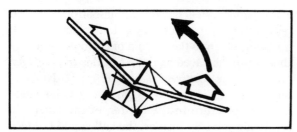

Fig. 2-43. Dihedral stability.

Where else can this load factor be a real problem? Right after takeoff, on climbout, you have an engine failure. The natural first reaction is to try to make it back to the runway. You have to make a tight turn, at a low airspeed, and without power. Mix all these together and you have a power-off *stall* going for you. Word of advice: *Land straight ahead in the event of engine failure on takeoff!*

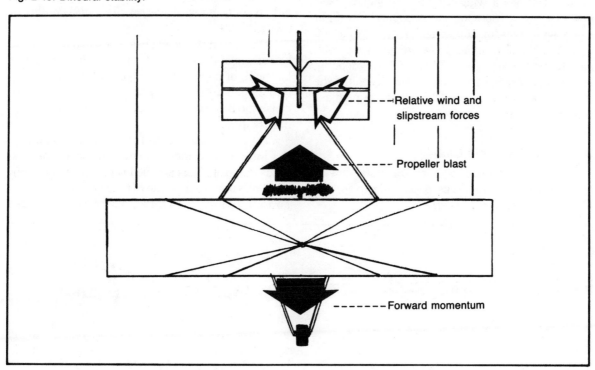

Fig. 2-44. The stability around the vertical axis due to the weathervaning effect.

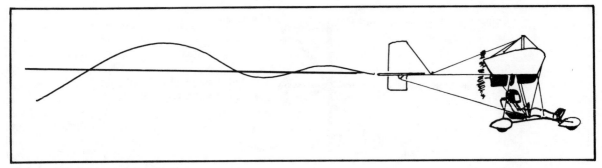

Fig. 2-45. Positive dynamic stability.

Wing Loading

When you multiply the wing span (tip to tip) times the chord (leading to trailing edge), you get *wing area*. Now, divide the wing area into the *weight* (gross) and you get the *wing loading*. To give you an idea of why the ultralight is so susceptible to winds and gusts, take a look. (To find wing area, again, the wingspan is multiplied by the chord.) A Cessna 152 has a wing area of 160 square feet; gross weight is 1600 pounds. A popular ultralight has a wing area of 160 square feet, GW is 400 pounds. (The ultralight's gross weight is a combination of pilot and plane.) The C152 wing loading is 10 pounds/square foot of wing surface while the ultralight's wing loading is 2.5 pounds per square foot of surface.

Static and Dynamic Stability

Stability is a form of equilibrium or steadiness. One of the best examples used to demonstrate stability is the "ball in a bowl."

Imagine a steel ball in a round-bottomed cereal bowl. No matter which way you displace the ball, it would return to the bottom of the bowl and stay there until displaced again. Keep this in mind: An object that is *positively stable* will resist displacement. Our ball is said to be positively stable since it tends to return to the bottom of the bowl. To carry this one step further, the ball would be *statically stable* since it would tend to return to its *original* position. So we have *positive static stability* in this example.

Okay, turn the bowl upside down and place the ball on top of the bowl at the peak of the curve. The ball will, of course, tend to roll off in almost any direction. This is called *negative static stability* because the ball has *no* tendency to return to its original position.

If you put the steel ball on a flat table, and give it a little displacement, it will roll for a short distance and stop. This is called *neutral static stability*.

Let's now apply some of these principles to the aircraft. In Figs. 2-45 through 2-47, we have three

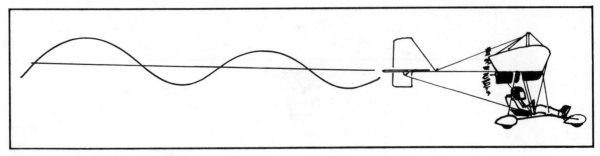

Fig. 2-46. Neutral dynamic stability.

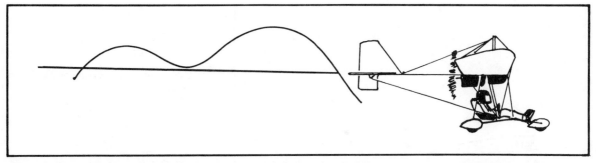

Fig. 2-47. This is an example of negative dynamic stability; the oscillations would increase in amplitude.

different reactions to displacement.

In Fig. 2-45, the ultralight exhibits a tendency to return to its original position by a series of diminishing oscillations. This would be an example of positive stability. The one big difference here is the craft is moving. Static stability (above) implies that the craft is not moving and when we have forward movement, this would be called *dynamic*. Rather than speak of an object returning to a static condition, consider that it has a tendency to return to its original position while moving. This would be called *dynamic stability*. Carrying it one step further, if as shown in Fig. 2-45 it tends to return to its original state while flying, it would be *positive dynamic stability*. The elevator would be the control surface that would be used to make the necessary pitch corrections.

If a force, such as a gust, displaces the aircraft from its original path, and the pilot doesn't fight the recovery, the craft returns to its original attitude because it is positively (dynamic) stable. This is a desirable form of stability along the pitch axis.

In Fig. 2-46 the aircraft, if displaced by a gust, just keeps on oscillating in equal modes. This kind of recovery is known as *neutral dynamic stability*. There is no increase or decrease in oscillations.

Stability in a Stall

Stalls are a part of life to the airman. When the airplane stalls, we want it to be docile and have no surprises. Essentially, we want the airplane to stall straight ahead, without dropping a wing, and we want the nose to fall predictably downward but not too far.

The best stall occurs from the wing root (near

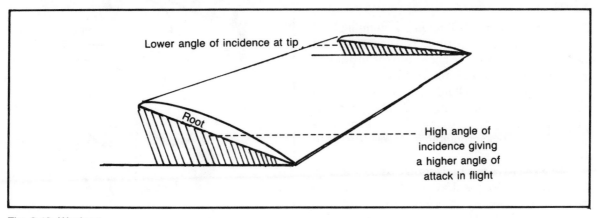

Lower angle of incidence at tip

Root

High angle of incidence giving a higher angle of attack in flight

Fig. 2-48. Washout.

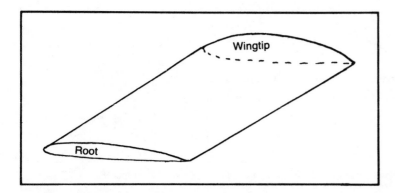

Fig. 2-49. Variation in the airfoil along the wingspan.

the kingpost), then progressing outward toward the wing tip. Here's how the manufacturers do it:

The wing may have a built-in twist designed to make the wing tip have a lower angle of incidence than the wing root. The difference is usually not much more than a few degrees. This twist is called *washout*; if the tips were of a *higher* angle of incidence, this would be called a *wash-in* (Fig. 2-48).

What all this amounts to is that the wing, with a lesser angle of incidence at the tips, would stall from root outward.

In a few cases, we might incorporate a spanwise airfoil variation, which means the wing tip would have a greater camber, giving it a stalling characteristic "later" than that of the root. This would in turn cause the tip to stall last (Fig. 2-49).

DRAG

Imagine you are walking in a swimming pool with water up to your beltline. You can easily feel the "drag" on your lower body, and the faster you try to move, the greater the resistance.

The drag that is pulling on your body is much like the drag that is constantly working against your ultralight when you're flying. Air is a mass of molecules, and when something moves through it, drag is created.

Drag comes in two basic forms: *parasite* and *induced*. *Parasite* drag is drag due to form such as wires, skin friction, and interference between components (Fig. 2-50). There are several contributing

factors to parasite drag. First, there is air density. The air is "thicker" at sea level than it would be at 33,000 feet. Area is another factor in drag. This is easily seen when a truck is compared to a Corvette. All of these factors are working against the ultralight, creating a resistance that has to be overcome by thrust. When thrust ceases, drag takes over and slows the aircraft down.

The other form of drag is known as *induced*. *Induced* drag is drag due to lift, and as the lift increases, so does the induced drag. Here is how it works: At the wing tips, air literally spills upward from the higher pressure on the underside to the lower pressure area on the upper side. This creates a *vortex* or "swirl" that follows the aircraft like a wake. In conventional aircraft terminology, it is re-

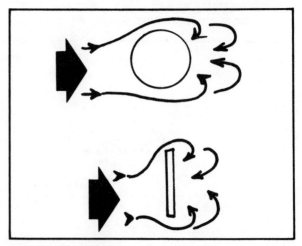

Fig. 2-50. Form drag.

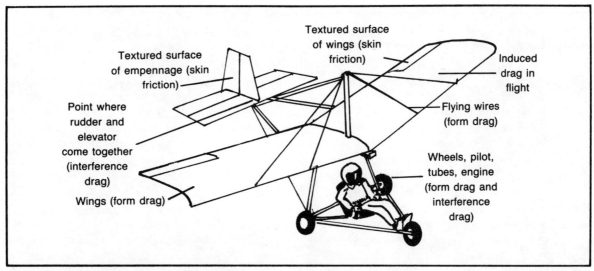

Fig. 2-51. Drag factors present in an ultralight.

ferred to as *wake turbulence*. You can see that if a swirl upward occurs, then the air inboard from the tip, on the underside, will move outward to fill the void. The whole underside of the wing air movement is shifted outward. The opposite occurs on the upper surface of the wing. The air shifts inboard and this total movement of air, bottom to top, creates a drag known as induced.

It should be noted that in the case of parasite drag, as the speed doubles, the drag quadruples.

In the case of induced drag, as the speed increases, the drag decreases. Enormous amounts of induced drag are created when a 747 is in a landing configuration.

An ultralight is a classic example of "drag in flight." Everywhere you look, you will find aerodynamic inefficiency (Fig. 2-51). However, the general consensus is, "Who cares?" The object is to have a fun-flying machine regardless of its efficiency.

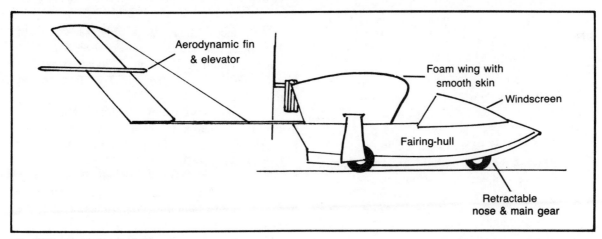

Fig. 2-52. Low-drag ultralight.

Fig. 2-53. Aerodynamic fairing around nose gear of a Quicksilver MX aircraft. These not only look good, they reduce drag!

The FAA in FAR Part 103, has also helped in putting a "lid" on efficiency with a speed limit for ultralights. Under applicability, it states " . . . is not capable of more than 55 knots calibrated airspeed at full power in level flight."

In 1980, I had the opportunity to attend the EAA Fly-In at Oshkosh; at that meet I saw what I consider to be one of the most beautiful aircraft ever conceived. The plane was the Osprey II, by George Pereira, of Sacramento, California.

Because of the "fairing-hull" and the retractable landing gear, it seems the amphibian would be the logical choice for a low-drag ultralight. With inspiration from the Osprey II, I have drawn a craft that would incorporate many drag reductions in its design (Figs. 2-52, 2-53).

GRAVITY

On the face of the Earth, all objects have weight and are pulled toward the center of the Earth. That seems easy enough; however, in aviation, we are given some terms that are more specific than just regular weight:

Empty weight is the empty weight of the aircraft including undrainable oil, if equipped, and undrainable fuel from lines, carburetor, and tank.

Gross weight is the maximum allowable weight for the aircraft as stated by the manufacturer.

Useful load is the gross weight minus the licensed empty weight, sometimes called the *payload.*

Most manufacturers of ultralights give you a

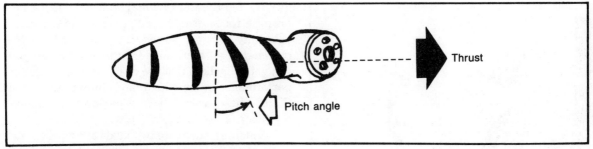

Fig. 2-54. Pitch variation along the propeller blade.

statement of the useful load their planes will carry. A lot depends upon the weight of the pilot and the amount of fuel that is on board. It is good piloting technique to know the useful load of the aircraft and always stay within the recommended limits of the manufacturer.

An overloaded aircraft is dangerous. Let me show you why. Although we haven't touched on this, the air temperature affects performance dramatically. If you happen to take off overloaded, it is quite possible the airplane will not climb out of its shadow. You see, the performance specs given for your aircraft are usually stated at sea level. When the temperature gets up during the day, the air thins out and has an *effective* altitude much higher than you actually are. This drop in performance due to air density is called *density altitude*. If the atmosphere is "high (altitude), hot (temp), and humid," look out; you may be in for real trouble.

An aircraft that is loaded far aft of the normal CG limit is very dangerous. If, for some reason, you would happen to get into a stall, there is a good possibility the aircraft would not recover, just flat spin back to earth. The reason is, of course, the center of gravity has to be ahead of the center of lift for a normal stall recovery. If the CG can't be made to swing forward of the center of gravity, the nose won't drop. The aircraft will fall like a leaf, or worse, start a rotation that is known as a *flat spin*.

An aircraft that is loaded far ahead of the CG limit is also dangerous and this is especially true when landing. It is quite possible for a pilot to "run out" of elevator during landing, trying to keep the nose up during a flare. If the aircraft is loaded ahead of the CG, it is possible to hit so hard, on landing, that the nose gear will collapse.

THRUST

A propeller is actually a wing that is lifting for-

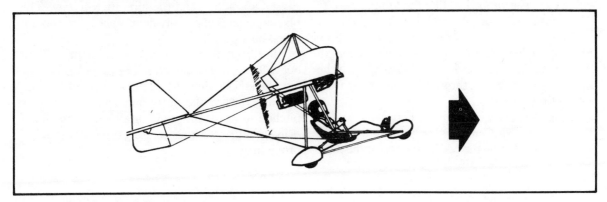

Fig. 2-55. P-factor on takeoff and climbout.

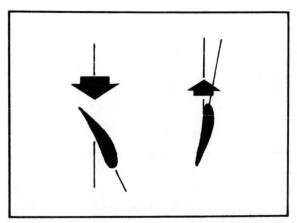

Fig. 2-56. Pitch angles of the propeller during high angles of attack.

ward. Propellers have leading and trailing edges, camber, angle of attack, relative wind, drag, and all the characteristics of a regular wing.

As the propeller rotates, the leading edge encounters the relative wind and this creates a "forward lift," only this lift is called *thrust*. If a condition is affecting normal wing lift, you can bet it's happening to your propeller. A classic example of this would be air that has been thinned due to heat or high altitude. If the wing efficiency decreases due to these and other factors, so does the propeller efficiency.

Make no mistake about it, like a wing, a propeller can be stalled. If the angle of attack of the propeller exceeds the critical angle of attack, a stall will occur. The propeller, like the wing, loses its aerodynamic efficiency and thrust decreases.

Look closely at the propeller and you will notice that the blade angle changes along the length of the propeller. This twist is necessary since the difference in the speed through the air varies from hub to tip (Fig. 2-54).

Propellers are a compromise between high and low pitch angles. Compare the prop to a bicycle with one sprocket on the pedals and one at the rear,

like the old-time Schwinn. The bicycle is a compromise for *most* riding situations. The propeller is usually designed so that it is efficient throughout *most* flight situations. On the other hand, you can get propellers that are designed to give better performance in the takeoff and climb profiles of a flight. These are called *climb propellers*. A regular propeller is called a *cruise* prop.

Generally, there are two kinds of propellers for conventional aircraft. One is a *fixed-pitch* and the other is *constant-speed*. The constant-speed does just that; it has a governor mechanism on it that is designed to keep the engine rpm at a constant rate, thus conserving both the engine and fuel.

Torque is a twisting force; in the case of the ultralight, the propeller provides this action by its rotation. As you are aware, for every action, there is an equal and opposite reaction. In this case, the aircraft has a tendency to rotate (reaction) in a direction opposite the rotation (action) of the propeller. Most aircraft have a built-in correction for torque.

P-factor occurs when the line of rotation is changed so that the descending blade of the propeller has a different angle of attack than the ascending blade. As the propeller rotates clockwise on the shaft, in straight and level flight, each blade gets an equal "bite" of the relative wind. Without changing the flight path, but increasing the angle of attack, the descending blade will also increase in angle of attack, or get a bigger bite than the upswinging blade. This bigger bite on the down blade causes a reaction and the aircraft will yaw. This phenomenon is especially noticeable on takeoff and climb-out.

In Fig. 2-55 we see how the ultralight in climb-out will experience P-factor. The propeller is rotating clockwise when viewed from behind (looking forward toward the nose) and when the nose is pitched upward, the angle of attack on the down blade gets greater, thus creating the P-factor torque problem (Fig. 2-56).

Chapter 3

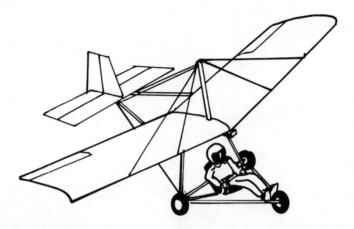

Ground Operations

The previously trained aviator has had "preflight" drilled into him since the very first "discovery" flight. It is an integral part of any flight training syllabus and a very important one at that.

It is quite possible for someone, without previous flight training, to buy an ultralight, new or used, transport it to a flight site, fly it, and (hopefully) return without ever going over the aircraft for safety reasons. Since flight training is not required and since the FAA doesn't require any aircraft registration, it is possible for this to become commonplace. Those of us already in the sport must make the newcomers aware of the importance of preflight safety inspections.

There are two characteristics of a good preflight: First, the preflight is performed in a consistent manner and it is done this same way every time, before every departure. Second, the preflight is always performed in an orderly manner. The pilot should start in a specific place and finish in a specific place.

THE CHECKLIST

One of the most important words to keep in mind when making a "walkaround" is *integrity*. When checking the integrity of a component, make sure that it is safe and airworthy. Checking the integrity of tubes means inspecting for dents, cuts, bends, scratches, etc. Would any of these faults affect the safety and integrity of the component, and, ultimately, the aircraft? Wire is another item that should be closely inspected; wires should be free of kinks and frays (Fig. 3-1).

Let's now take a closer look at an organized checklist that should prove valuable to ALL ultralight aircraft.

1. First, check all controls by moving the control stick. If the aircraft has a variable CG seat arrangement, move the seat around and watch the control surfaces that are attached (Fig. 3-2).
2. Make sure the connections that link the

Fig. 3-1. The integrity of every component should be checked in the preflight inspection.

control surfaces with the control stick are secure and pinned where applicable.

3. Check the movement of the elevator and notice its "feel." It should not be binding anywhere in its full travel.

4. Check the rudder and rudder pedals to make sure the movement is not binding up. If the aircraft is equipped with spoilerons, these should be operating free and the return cords should make the spoilerons "snap" back into position (Fig. 3-3).

5. The pilot should go to each control pulley at this time and check to make sure the cable, or cord, is moving freely in the pulley.

6. The pilot's seat should be checked to make sure it is bolted securely to the seat down

tube, or if it is a variable CG model, the attachments should be checked to make sure nothing will come loose in flight.

7. The seat downtubes should be checked where they are attached (example would be the root tube attachment).

8. The nose wire or nose tube should be carefully checked for attachment and integrity.

9. The nose gear should be checked, including the foot bar, tension struts, and connecting hardware.

10. The triangle bar corner clusters of wire and all necessary fitting attachments should be checked. This inspection should include the triangle bar tubes.

11. The leading edge spars should be checked

Fig. 3-2. Control surfaces should be checked at the cockpit as well as at the point of attachment.

the tail booms, if applicable.

16. Check the gear reduction unit and make sure the belts are at the proper tension.

17. Check the integrity of the tail booms and all attachments. This is a very critical part of the aircraft and one should be careful not to miss any attachment.

18. Visually check the kingpost and all of the cable attachments.

19. Check the leading edge of the stabilizer and elevator attachment points.

20. Check the trailing edge of the stabilizer. The hinge points where the elevator attaches should be double checked and the elevator push-pull tube assembly and at-

including wires, wire attachment points, and sailcloth at the wing's leading edge.

12. Aileron control arms, cords, and control surface should be checked.

13. The trailing edge spar should be checked on the wing being inspected. This includes the wire attachments and individual cables.

14. Check attachment points of the empennage at the stabilizer's edge. Make sure pins are in place and secure.

15. Now check the propeller attachment bolts and make sure the prop isn't cracked or excessively chipped along or near the leading edges. Check the propeller gear reduction belt(s). Make sure the tips clear

Fig. 3-3. The pilot should examine all attachments, cables and components by touching. A written checklist is strongly advised.

Fig. 3-4. Helmets are a must for safety. Get one and wear it!

tachment should be checked.

21. At this time, the rudder should be carefully inspected and all attachment points should be checked.
22. Any cables attached to the empennage should be checked at this time.
23. The opposite (from the one just checked) wing should now be thoroughly checked; this would include the cables, ailerons, all attachments, leading and trailing edge spars and sailcloth.
24. Finally, the root tube should be carefully checked for integrity.
25. The pilot should now go over the engine:
    a. Fuel line including clamps.
    b. Fuel filter and crossover.

c. Starter cable and handle.
d. Spark plug and wire attachments, including kill switch.
e. Mounting bolts and other hardware.
26. Parachute attachment and overall appearance.
27. Helmet on and adjusted (Fig. 3-4).
28. Movement of controls.
29. Finally, a visual check of fuel quantity. Look closely for any visible signs of contamination such as water or dirt.

TAXIING

Since ground handling is so very important in the ultralight, it is good piloting technique to master the taxi art before going much farther.

The student pilot should practice all taxiing in a large open area that allows experience to be gained by some experimentation.

Problem areas for the first-time student pilot usually boil down to overcontrolling. First, the rookie will have a tendency to bring the power on full, only to find that the aircraft moves too rapidly; the student senses this acceleration and abruptly backs off the power and the aircraft comes to a halt or slows down to a point where no directional control remains. The power needed to get the aircraft moving is called *breakaway thrust*. If you will watch a pilot with a lot of experience, you will find that he brings the power up with finesse; once a desired level of forward motion is attained, just enough power is maintained to keep the aircraft moving briskly. If you will compare this to teaching your little brother to drive a car with a clutch, you will immediately see what I mean. The initial tendency is to let the clutch out too quickly and the car lurches forward, and sometimes dies. Once you have screamed at the kid four or five times, he soon learns to bring the power in nice and steady while letting the clutch engage slowly. After awhile, it becomes a smooth transition from stop to go.

The ultralight aircraft with a fixed nose gear is directionally controlled on the ground by a blast of air against the rudder. This means the more air

Fig. 3-5. Turn aircraft away from spectators. The engine/propeller blast needed to make the rudder effective can also throw rocks and debris.

you have passing over the rudder, the more effective the rudder becomes in turning the aircraft.

Even with the rudder in full right or left deflection, the only other variable would be the velocity of the airflow over the control surface. There are two ways of getting a greater amount of airflow

over the rudder: Obviously, you can increase power thus increasing thrust; secondly, you can taxi faster. The recommended procedures for turning are:

☐ **Nosewheel aircraft**—Pull the stick aft, deflect the rudder in the direction you want

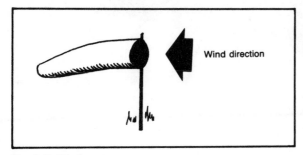

Fig. 3-6. Wind sock.

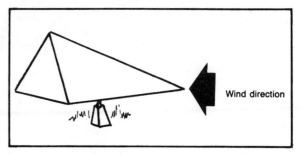

Fig. 3-7. Tetrahedron.

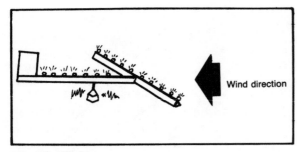

Fig. 3-8. Wind tee.

to turn, and increase thrust.

☐ **Tailwheel aircraft**—Push stick slightly forward, deflect the rudder and increase the thrust.

Be aware that with a fast taxi, you may reach a speed that is sufficient to become airborne!

If your aircraft is equipped with ailerons, there is a recommended procedure for taxi in a crosswind. If the wind is from the front, *fly into the wind*

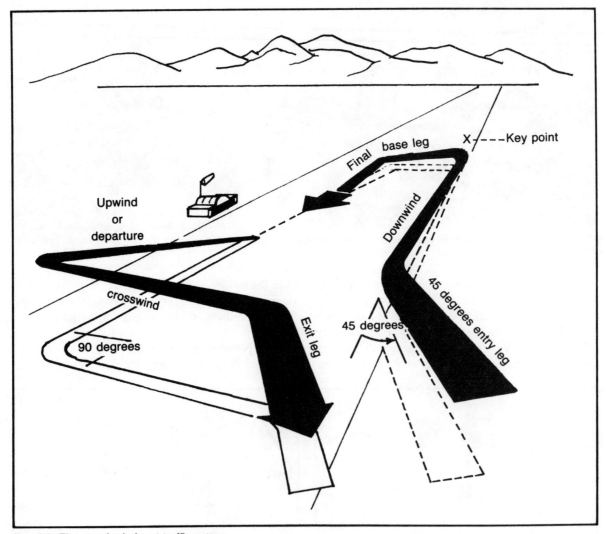

Fig. 3-9. The standard airport traffic pattern.

with the controls; that is, right stick for a right front wind, left stick for a left front wind. If the wind is from the rear of the aircraft, *fly away from the wind*; again, that is, wind from right rear, apply left stick and if wind is from the left rear, apply right stick.

The Importance of Planning Ahead

The best technique for a safe taxi is to plan ahead. If the aircraft has the tractor-type propeller (prop out front), planning is essential. Why? With a reduced propeller blast to the rudder, the pilot must carefully position the aircraft so that the greatest amount of prop blast gives directional control without posing an undue blast hazard to spectators (Fig. 3-5).

When analyzing techniques, consider the terrain's grade and surface. Is it paved? Is it grass? Is it rocky or rough? Is it uphill or downhill? Is it muddy or dry? Once you become aware of conditions, think about what it is going to be like before you taxi out.

It stands to reason that when you are moving across a grass field with a downhill grade, your taxi is going to be "fast." It might be compared to a golf ball on a putting green. If you are going to have to turn 90 degrees on a slippery surface in a fast taxi to get rudder control, you may be far from your selected takeoff point by the time you figure out you have a problem.

Taxiing in the Wind

In your imagination, look back at the rudder. Notice how large the surface area is; now look at the distance between the rudder and the center of gravity. Any wind from any direction other than straight ahead or directly behind the aircraft is go-ing to have a definite affect on your taxi. The wind is going to "weathercock" the aircraft even if you are taxiing directly into it. If the wind is sufficient in force, it can ground loop the aircraft, or worse, if could get under your wing and flip the aircraft on its back.

Taxiing from a crosswind heading to a downwind heading will result in a larger radius of turn at any given speed. Since the wind constantly wants to weathercock the craft into the wind, the pilot must constantly be fighting the force (Figs. 3-6 through 3-8).

When making a turn from a downwind to an upwind heading, the pilot should be especially careful. The problem is in a ground loop; not only do you have the force of the wind to contend with, you have centrifugal force acting upon the aircraft. In this ground loop, the aircraft may literally "bank" as it is turning. Naturally, it banks to the outside and this in turn may allow some of the wind to ge under the wing. You can see that if the force of the wind is strong enough, the downwind wing may strike the ground; in cases where the force is sufficient, the aircraft may be flipped over.

Sudden, short bursts of power will give a desirable rate of turn without a penalty of increased speed or increased radius of turn. The big factor here is to get the air blast over the rudder without the momentum of the aircraft building up to dangerous levels.

Taxiing to the Active Runway

Before moving on to a runway, it is good practice to look around to make sure that no aircraft is coming at you on the ground and that you are not going to interfere with someone else in the final approach phase of their landing (Fig. 3-9).

Chapter 4

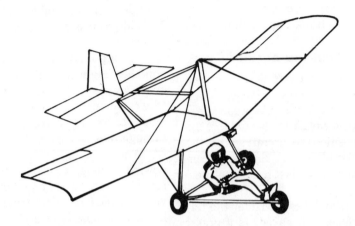

The Ultralight in Flight

The aircraft is taxied onto the active runway and it is brought into perfect alignment with the centerline of the runway. It is important that the vision of the pilot be aimed at a distant point at the end of the runway and not at a point somewhere directly in front of the aircraft (Fig. 4-1).

The reason for this is the overall sense of awareness of the takeoff and any deviations necessary when the takeoff sequence begins. If the pilot is aware of the overall picture, changes can be made, when necessary, before a problem develops. Crosswinds are a classic example of this. If a crosswind component changes as you are taking off, the change will be noticed immediately and corrections can be made.

THE TAKEOFF SEQUENCE

Full power should be developed as early as practical in the takeoff sequence. Some pilots keep their feet on the ground and bring the engine up to full power before starting the roll. This procedure gives the pilot a chance to "test" the engine

to see that it is developing full power. However, it should be noted that it is far safer to have someone assist you in the engine test. On the Eipper Quicksilver and some other aircraft, if your leg slips under the aircraft accidentally you can not only hurt yourself, but also break the teleflex cable tube that is hooked to the rudder. If someone else is helping, and the power doesn't seem to be up to full, adjustments can be made before takeoff is attempted.

Again, the power should be brought to full only when you are fully ready to initiate the takeoff sequence. One final "lookaround" has to be made so that no other persons, aircraft, or onlookers are going to become a problem.

The Takeoff Roll

As full power is applied and the ultralight starts to roll, you should remember that your directional control is accomplished by rudder deflection. Even if the aircraft is equipped with individual main wheel brakes, it is not a good idea to use these on

Fig. 4-1. Aiming point at the beginning of the takeoff roll.

takeoff or landing. Pitch control is not effective until you reach about 15 miles per hour on most ultralights; therefore, your elevator doesn't do that much good in the beginning.

If the pilot were to pull the control stick full aft during takeoff, the aircraft would most likely climb into the ground effect with a very high nose attitude, then stall and return to the runway. Most instructors recommend that you hold a neutral stick until flying speed is reached, then a very slight back pressure to increase the angle of attack. The craft will literally fly itself into the air. You can get a good idea of the angle of attack you have when you rotate by having your instructor hold down on the tail of the aircraft while you're sitting up front in the seat. The nose wheel should come about six inches off the ground and that's where it will be, approximately, when you start to become airborne (Figs. 4-2, 4-3).

At a given airspeed—usually around 30 miles per hour—the aircraft will come off the ground and start climbing. It is desirable to make the craft climb at an angle that gives good forward visibility and also doesn't put a strain on the engine. There are two climb out airspeeds that are com-

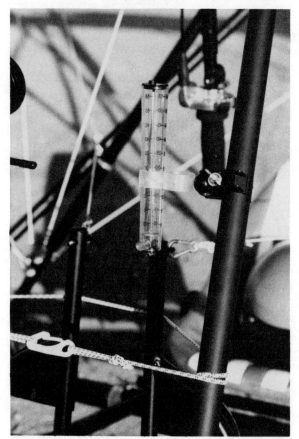

Fig. 4-2. Your airspeed indicator is a very important instrument.

monly used. First you have the *best angle of climb* airspeed; this is defined as the airspeed that results in the greatest increase in altitude with respect to the distance over the ground. The second is the *best rate of climb* airspeed; this airspeed gives the maximum increase in altitude in a unit of time only.

Previously trained pilots may have difficulty with the lack of horizontal references; in an ultralight, about the only thing you have in front of you is your feet! This loss of a frame of reference is most disconcerting. Almost from the very beginning of flight training a student pilot is taught to use the nose of the aircraft for maneuvers involving takeoffs, turns, climbs, descents, landings, etc. Most general aviation instructors will find a rookie student looking at the wingtips and will immediately tell the student not to use them as a reference. However, in ultralight flying, just the opposite applies. The ultralight pilot *must* use the wingtips for reference; that is about all that is available, other than the feet. One of the nice things about the transition from powered aircraft to ultralights is that the previously trained pilot expects something different! Therefore, all of the references previously used can be changed without undue psychological stress on the pilot. It goes without saying this is an "attitude" change more than anything else. Since the pilot is aware that ultralights are different, the mind is better able to cope with the change. If the pilot would feel more comfortable with a reference, a dowel rod can be taped to a down tube until the kinesthetic sense is developed.

CLIMBOUT

Thirty to 35 miles per hour is about the best rate of climb airspeed for some popular ultralights. The first turn is made at approximately 150 feet above ground level (AGL), and in keeping with standardized procedures, the turn will be made to the left (Fig. 4-4).

In Fig. 4-5, you can see how a climbing turn looks from the cockpit. Climbing turns are made at shallow bank angles. Remember the stall speed increases as the angle of bank increases. In a climb,

Fig. 4-3. The moment of truth—it flies!

your speeds are relatively low and a steep bank could stall the aircraft. Another reason for shallow turns in a climb is the loss of lift and subsequent reduction in the rate of climb. The whole idea is to gain altitude; therefore, if you bank the aircraft too much, you're defeating the purpose.

Pattern Exit

After a short climb on the crosswind leg, you will make a shallow right bank and turn to a heading which is 45 degrees to the crosswind heading. This is the standard pattern exit used by general aviation aircraft (Fig. 4-6).

If you find your climb to be sluggish, you may be encountering the effect of *density altitude*. Den-

sity altitude is sometimes called the "effective altitude" since it is the condition of the atmosphere at the time of the flight. Three conditions affect the atmosphere in a density altitude situation and the ultralight pilot should know them: the temperature, the altitude where you're flying, and the humidity. A good way to remember them is "high, hot, and humid!" What happens is this: When the air is warmed, it thins out and a decrease in the density occurs. If the air is already thin due to a high elevation, it can really have a detrimental effect on performance of the aircraft. Since water vapor displaces dry air molecules, humidity becomes a factor. The presence of humidity also means a decrease in air density. If the humidity is high enough,

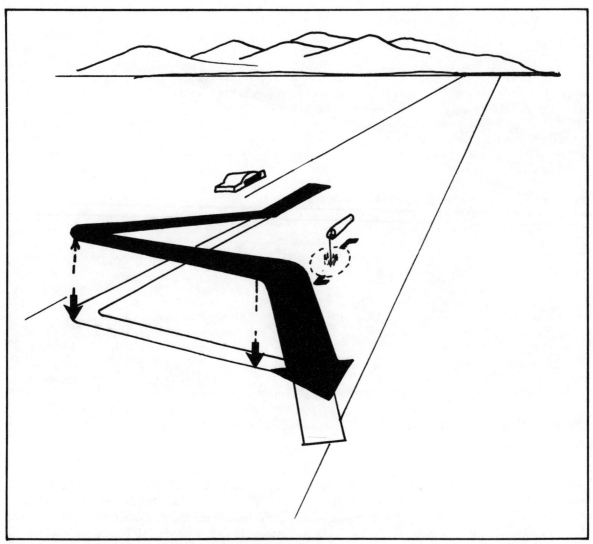

Fig. 4-4. The departure pattern used by general aviation aircraft.

it becomes a problem not only to the performance of the wing, but to the engine and propeller as well.

It is not uncommon for an ultralight to get off the ground in less than 150 feet, in the fall and winter, at elevations such as one would find in Colorado. However, at the peak of summer, I've seen the same ultralight take as much as a quarter of a mile to get airborne. You just don't have the same number of molecules per unit volume in the

summer as you have in the winter when the temperature is at or below standard. If the temperature is above standard where you're flying, be especially cautious in takeoff and landing.

Climb Aerodynamics

The lift in a normal climb is the same as in level flight at a given airspeed. With respect to climb, when the nose is raised, there is a momentary increase in lift, but the power has to be added to sustain the climb, otherwise the airspeed will bleed off. However, when the climb path and the angle of attack align, the forces of lift, drag, thrust and gravity come into equilibrium.

If one of the forces is increased or decreased, the results will be either an acceleration or a deceleration.

AIRSPEED

If your ultralight does not have an airspeed indicator, it is advisable to get one (Fig. 4-7). Airspeed is *extremely* important to the pilot. Knowledge of airspeed is critical to takeoff, climb, stalls, descent, approach, and landing.

There are four different kinds of airspeed and the pilot should know the differences. First, when

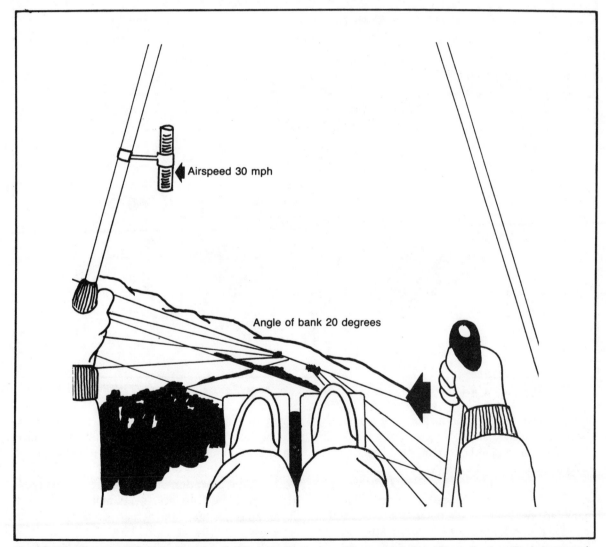

Airspeed 30 mph

Angle of bank 20 degrees

Fig. 4-5. Climbing turn to the left after takeoff. This is the beginning of the crosswind leg. Normally, the altitude is approximately 150 feet above the ground.

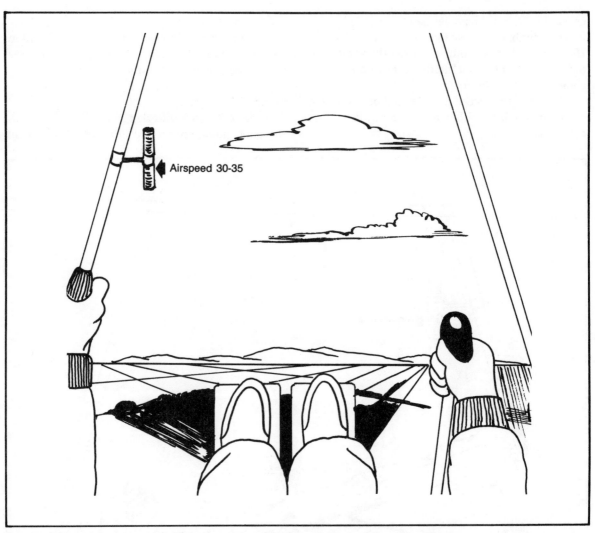

Fig. 4-6. Pattern exit at a 45 degree angle to the crosswind; altitude is approaching 200 feet.

you look at the airspeed indicator, you are observing the *indicated airspeed*. Indicated airspeed is uncorrected for any other error such as density, instrument and etc. *True airspeed* is the actual speed of the aircraft through the air mass. *Calibrated* airspeed is the indicated airspeed corrected for instrument and position errors. *Groundspeed* is the actual speed of the craft across the earth. In other words, it is the speed of your shadow at high noon!

You should be aware of the fact that when the air mass is thin, as you would find when the density altitude is high, the airspeed indicator will give an indication much lower than the actual airspeed of the craft. Here's an example: On a 25° C day, with a flight elevation of 4900 feet, the density altitude would be 7140 feet. If your indicated airspeed is 40 miles per hour, the actual speed through the air mass would be 44 mph. This is an example of true airspeed, since it is airspeed corrected for temperature and altitude.

An airspeed indicator becomes quite inaccurate near a stall. When the air is hitting the indicator hole, or pitot tube inlet at an angle, the ram pressure will be altered. This means that as the angle of attack is increased and the airspeed is low, you cannot rely upon the reading of the airspeed indicator.

It has been said that straight and level flight is a series of corrections to keep the aircraft in that attitude; in essence, this is quite true. Your control inputs should be made with finesse; jerkiness should be avoided. Smooth operation is a sign of good piloting technique and this habit should be established early in your flying career.

TURNS

First let's take a look at the dynamics of a turn, then we'll get into the technique. Figure 4-8 shows the forces in a conventional turn at a constant altitude. It is interesting to note that a turn is one

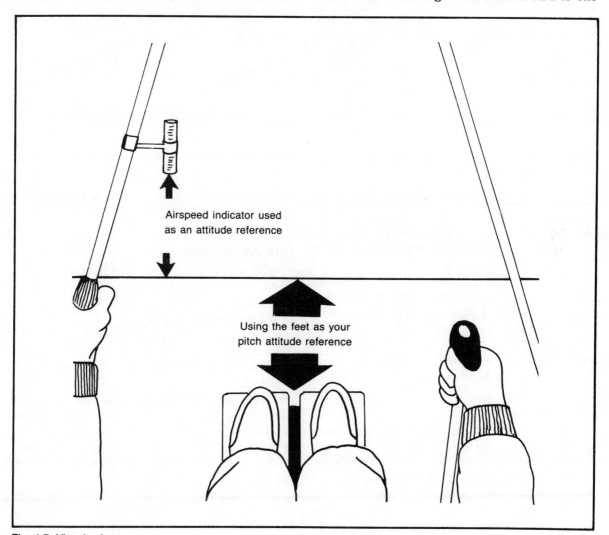

Fig. 4-7. Visual references.

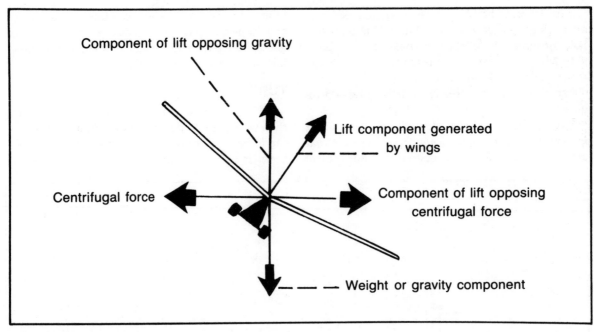

Fig. 4-8. Lift forces in a turn.

maneuver where lift must be greater than weight. The reason is the presence of centrifugal force and its tendency to keep the aircraft from turning. A portion of the generated lift is necessary to oppose this force.

When an aircraft banks, part of the lift component is wrong. Centrifugal force enters the picture and a component of lift is needed to offset this influence. If the pilot makes no correction for this loss of lift, a subsequent loss of altitude will occur. Increasing the angle of attack is necessary to keep from losing altitude when banking the aircraft.

Turning Technique

Before making a turn, *look around*. Some other aircraft may be very close to you. If your wing is blocking the view, a turn in that direction may result in a mid-air collision. Be like a fighter pilot and keep that head moving.

To make the turn, simply move the control stick in the direction of the turn and give a gentle back pressure at the same time. Not only are you

initiating roll, you are increasing the angle of attack (Fig. 4-9).

Turn Aerodynamics

Although your particular aircraft may have conventional three-axis controls, the following narrative and illustration will describe the set-up found on the Eipper Quicksilver MX.

In making a right turn, the movement of the control stick will deflect the rudder to the right as shown in Fig. 4-10. This yaws the aircraft around the lateral axis and the left wing will encounter the relative wind at a higher velocity than the right wing. As a result, a greater lift is produced on the left wing. The greater lift raises the left wing and produces a right bank. Since the rudder is deflected to the right, the effects of adverse yaw are minimized.

Making a turn to the left is exactly the same procedure (Fig. 4-11). Simply move the stick from its neutral position to the left. When the desired angle of bank is reached, neutralize the stick and the aircraft will maintain that angle.

If the pilot keeps moving the stick toward the direction of bank, the aircraft will roll inverted or spiral downward.

Overbanking

Many ultralight manufacturers build an angle into the wing that makes the wingtips higher than the root tube. This angle is called the *dihedral*. The

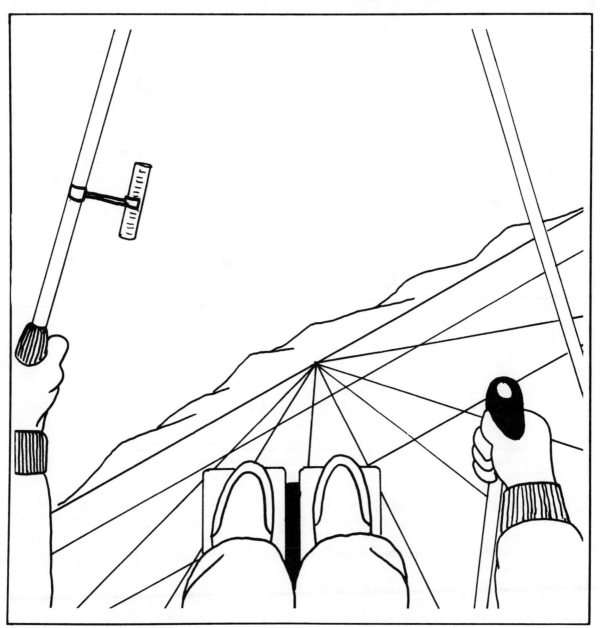

Fig. 4-9. Thirty degree bank to the right.

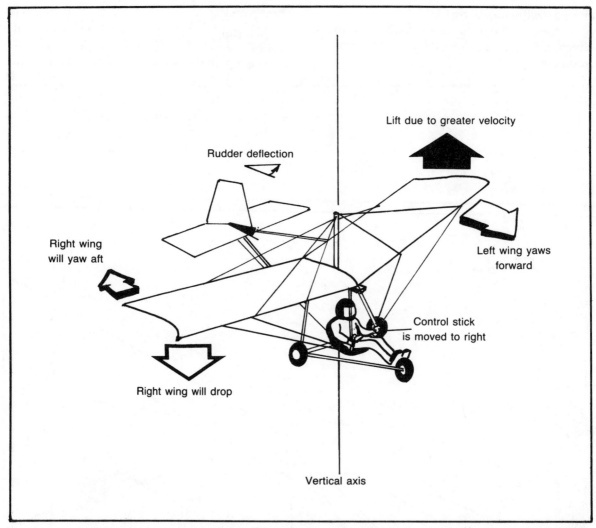

Lift due to greater velocity

Rudder deflection

Right wing
will yaw aft

Left wing yaws
forward

Control stick
is moved to right

Right wing will drop

Vertical axis

Fig. 4-10. Forces that make the aircraft bank right when the rudder or control stick is moved to the right (depending upon the type of aircraft.)

higher the dihedral, the more stable the aircraft will be along the longitudinal axis. This is all well and good, except the aircraft may be so stable that it will tend to "fight" the pilot in a shallow banked turn. In some cases, the pilot may have to overbank the aircraft to get the desired turn. Up to a point, this is no real problem; however, at bank angles of more than 60 degrees, the aircraft may have a tendency to overbank by itself.

As the angle of bank is increased, the wing to the outside of the turn will move faster, into the relative wind, than the inside wing. This subsequent increase in velocity will also create an increase in lift. The increase in lift may overbank the aircraft and, if not corrected, put the aircraft in a spiral since the nose tends to drop in the turn. If the airspeed builds up, the pilot may be in what is known as the "Graveyard Spiral."

Load Factors in a Turn

Another problem in banked turns of more than 30 degrees is the centrifugal force. Using a load factor chart, Fig. 4-12, you can see that only 1.15 Gs are "pulled" in a 30 degree bank. However, as the bank increases, the load factor goes up quite rapidly. In a 60 degree banked turn, the aircraft is pulling 2 Gs, or double the weight on the wings.

Rollout

Student pilots usually have two basic problems with turn rollouts. First, there is the problem of let-

ting the nose pitch up since the student fails to release the back pressure on the stick. Second, the student pilot tends to overshoot the heading and then S-turn to achieve the desired bearing.

The correct technique is to start the rollout ahead of the desired course by a sufficient margin that will allow the aircraft to have that heading when the wings are level.

STALLS

Stalls should be practiced to develop skills in the recognition and recovery of this maneuver.

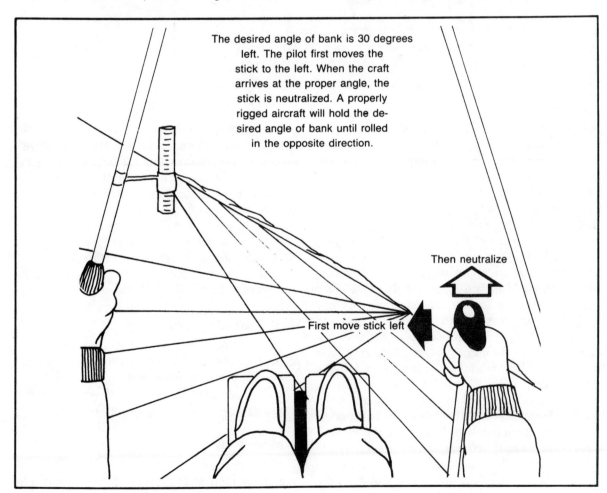

The desired angle of bank is 30 degrees left. The pilot first moves the stick to the left. When the craft arrives at the proper angle, the stick is neutralized. A properly rigged aircraft will hold the desired angle of bank until rolled in the opposite direction.

Then neutralize

First move stick left

Fig. 4-11. Thirty degree bank to the left.

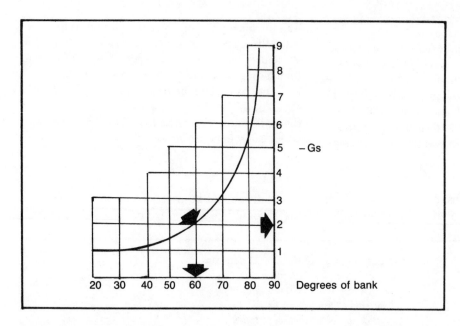

Fig. 4-12. Load factor chart.

Most people don't realize it, but the stall is an integral part of the normal landing. When the aircraft lands, the pilot attempts to make the plane stall just when the wheels touch the runway. In this way, the aircraft will make contact with the earth at its slowest flying speed.

During the practice of a stall, the pilot should become acutely aware of the cues that signal an *imminent* stall. Some of these cues are as follows.

In the ultralight, you'll note a *lack of wind pressure* when you are approaching a stall. This cue, of course, would apply to a straight-ahead stall such as the approach-to-landing-stall maneuver. Not only will the wind pressure be less, the *tone level* and *sound* intensity will decrease as the stall approaches. The pilot may even hear a fluttering noise as the burbling vibration occurs on the flying surfaces.

The sensing of a change in direction and the speed of motion is probably one of the best indicators of an imminent stall. The sensing phenomenon is known as *kinesthesia*, sometimes referred to as the "seat-of-the-pants" flying capability. If the sensitivity is properly developed, it will warn the pilot of a speed decrease and the beginning of a

sink, or altitude loss.

The feeling of a *change in control pressure* is also quite apparent. As the speed is reduced, the "live" resistance on the control stick becomes progressively less. The pressures on the stick soon become movements just to make effective changes in the control surfaces.

The practice of stall recovery is important especially in the development of an awareness of an imminent stall. Although this is not a specific kind of stall, it is important to know how to recognize and recover before the full stall occurs.

Stall Characteristics

The factors that affect the stall characteristics of an ultralight are: balance, attitude, bank angle, power applications, drag, and pilot coordination. The ultralight pilot should learn these effects and how they relate to aircraft being flown.

Imminent Stalls

The imminent stall, again, is one that is defined as an impending stall. Practice of this maneuver is primarily for retaining control of the aircraft upon

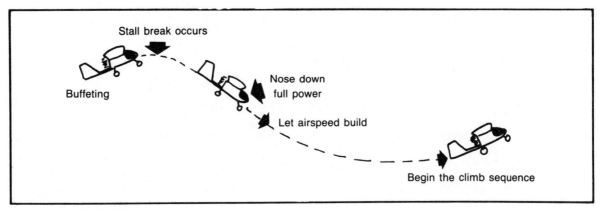

Stall break occurs

Buffeting

Nose down
full power

Let airspeed build

Begin the climb sequence

Fig. 4-13. The stall profile.

recognition of a full stall.

Imminent stall practice is valuable also because it develops the pilot's sense of feel for the maneuvers in which the maximum aircraft performance is required. In this maneuver, the recovery is initiated *before* the full stall is allowed to develop. When the buffet is noted, the angle of attack is reduced immediately and full power* is simultaneously applied. The pilot must learn to recognize the indications of the imminent stall and take positive and immediate action to prevent the full stall.

Stall Techniques

The practice of power-off stalls is usually done in wide-open areas and at altitudes above 1000 feet above ground level. *Before executing any stall maneuver, the pilot should clear the area of other aircraft.* There are several types of stalls and your instructor may or may not show you all of them.

The type we'll discuss is the approach-to-landing stall. This simulates a stall that would occur on approach when the pilot tries to abort a landing and stalls the aircraft doing so.

The pilot, before executing the stall maneuver, should clear the area of other aircraft. The altitude is held constant and the airspeed sustained at about

30 to 35 miles per hour. The power is then reduced to about 25 percent and the aircraft maneuvered into an approach attitude. As the airspeed bleeds off, the nose is raised smoothly to increase the angle of attack to the critical angle of attack.

One should be aware that if the nose is raised too abruptly, an *accelerated maneuver stall* may occur. This type of stall occurs from excessive maneuvering loads being imposed on the airframe.

The correct procedure is to bring the stick back smoothly and maintain directional control with the rudder. The rudder will not be stalled since it is not affected by the same angle of attack as the wing and elevator.

Many people think a stall is a violent maneuver that occurs with great altitude losses. In an ultralight, it usually doesn't happen this way at all. The stall is more than likely a mush or "near-stall" that occurs with very little loss of altitude.

If the aircraft is allowed to stall and the back pressure is not released, a wing may drop and the nose may pitch down quite a bit. However, if a normal stall recovery is initiated, the craft is usually very docile.

Normal recovery is made by first releasing back pressure on the stick to lower the nose, then applying power. Power is added to keep from losing too much altitude after the stall occurs (Figs. 4-13 through 4-17).

The true indication that an aircraft has reached

*Please refer to the individual manufacturer's handbook. Some ultralights should not use full power during recovery from a stall.

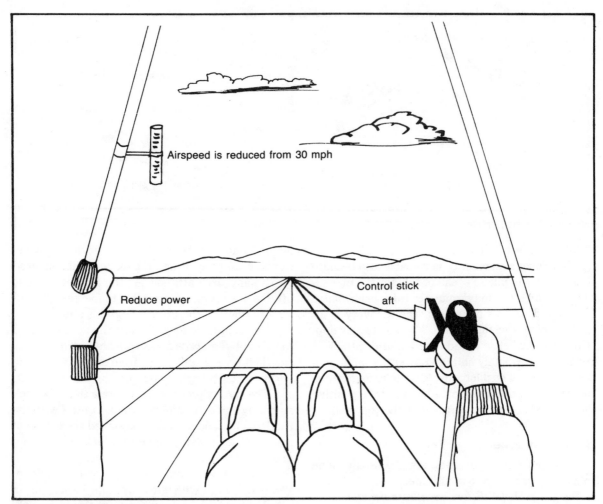

Airspeed is reduced from 30 mph

Reduce power

Control stick aft

Fig. 4-14. Initiating a stall.

the critical angle of attack is the buffeting. This vibration occurs as the burbling air starts to break away from the upper curved surfaces of the wing. The pilot should recognize this as the time to begin the recovery sequence.

Once the aircraft starts downward and power has been applied, the pullup can be started. However, the pullup should not be made too quickly since a *secondary stall* may occur. The airspeed should be allowed to build to what is known as "flying speed," or about 30 to 35 miles per hour in most ultralights.

The next step, after achieving a stabilized rate of descent, is the initiation of the *climb sequence*. The climb sequence is very important since it trains the pilot in the necessity of making a follow-through after the stall has occurred. The pilot should climb at about 30 to 35 miles per hour, or that airspeed needed for the best rate of climb. If the pilot has this airspeed, a successful go-around can be made, and full recovery is only a matter of repeating the procedure used in the climbout phase after takeoff.

In a power-on stall, the pilot will enter this maneuver from cruise, only the power will not be reduced as in the power-off stall. The nose is brought back until the aircraft's wing reaches the critical angle of attack. This may be somewhat alarming to the pilot since the nose will be considerably higher in pitch angle than in the power-off stall. When the aircraft stalls, the nose will drop and the pilot pushes the stick forward to decrease the angle of attack and brings in power, if needed, to regain level flight.

It should be remembered that the rudder of the aircraft is operable in a stall. This control surface will allow the pilot to have yaw control and thus be able to keep the aircraft from spinning. The rudder control allows the pilot to keep the same heading, and to a degree, the wings level in the stall. It should be noted that all control inputs at or near the stall are sloppy.

The ailerons (if your aircraft is so equipped) will be affected when the aircraft is stalled. The most desirable type of training ultralight would have stall characteristics that make the wing stall from the root tube outward toward the wingtips in a very

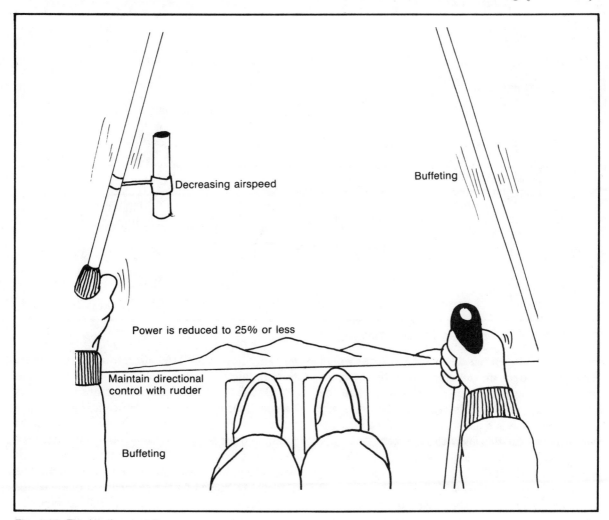

Fig. 4-15. The imminent stall.

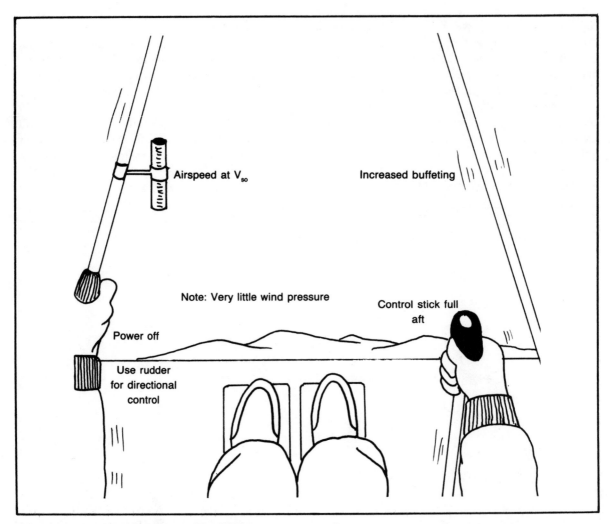

Fig. 4-16. Full stall from straight and level flight.

predictable way. In this design, the ailerons would have some effect on roll right up to the moment when the wing finally stalls. However, when the critical angle of attack is reached, the boundary layer separation and subsequent burbling also disturbs the air flowing over the ailerons.

As pointed out previously, although the ailerons and elevator are stalled, the rudder is not. The pilot should use the rudder with finesse during a stall so as not to aggrevate the situation and initiate a spin entry. Have a competent flight instructor show

you first how to stall the aircraft using the rudder to maintain directional control.

One factor that enters the picture in a stall is torque. This is especially significant in a power-on stall. Any time the nose reaches a high angle of pitch, and the wing is in a high angle of attack, the P-factor forces enter the picture and the aircraft wants to yaw in reaction to the torque force. The P-factor is caused by the descending blade of the propeller getting a bigger bite of the air than the ascending blade and thus causing an assymetrical thrust on one side of the propeller. The aircraft will yaw in the opposite direction, and if the pilot has put the plane in a stall entry, opposite rudder may have to be applied steadily to counteract the propeller forces.

Common Student Problems in Stall Maneuvers

In the early stages of flight training, students usually have problems with certain phases of stall maneuvers.

Problems with entry are:

☐ Letting the nose drop.
☐ Raising the nose too quickly and getting an accelerated stall.
☐ Not raising the nose high enough and never reaching a stall.

Problems with recovery are:

☐ Lowering the nose too much.

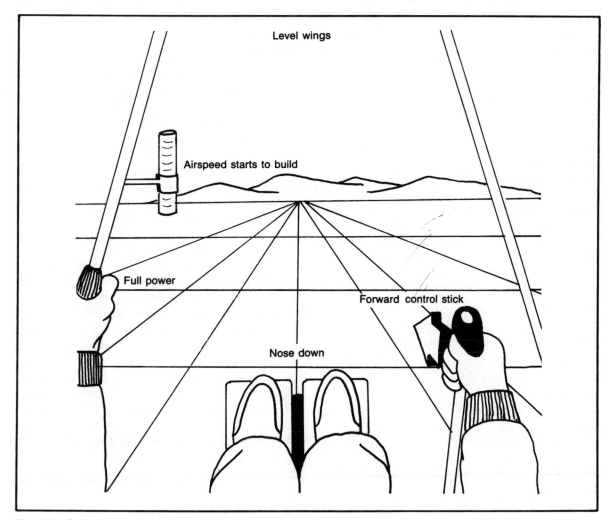

Level wings

Airspeed starts to build

Full power

Forward control stick

Nose down

Fig. 4-17. Stall recovery.

☐ Losing too much altitude in the recovery.
☐ Not adding power.
☐ Too rapid a recovery and getting a secondary stall.
☐ Not allowing airspeed to build to flying speed.

Slow Flight

Slow flight, or maneuvering at minimum controllable airspeed, will help a pilot build proficiency in learning to control the aircraft at airspeeds just above a stall. This is very important since the ultralight has a very narrow margin between minimum and maximum flying speed. Turns in slow flight teach the pilot to maintain altitude very near a stall yet make a change in direction. It should be noted that turns in slow flight are very shallow.

To begin the maneuver, the throttle is gradually reduced while the altitude is sustained with angle of attack. When the airspeed reaches the minimum controllable, the pilot should hold that attitude to keep the aircraft from stalling. Power adjustments should be made carefully and any pitch changes should be made without a gain or loss in altitude. In some aircraft an attempt to climb at such a slow speed may result in a loss of altitude. This is known as the *region of reverse command*. If the aircraft happens to stall, simply execute the standard recovery of putting the nose down and adding power.

GROUND REFERENCE MANEUVERS

The object of any ground reference maneuver is to develop piloting skill and learn to put the aircraft exactly where you want it. The ground reference maneuver is essential in polishing coordination and control touch. The pilot will soon learn to control the aircraft with a sense of the wind and what it is doing to the aircraft.

Some maneuvers are performed at relatively low altitudes; therefore the pilot should be especially careful in the selection of a practice area. Try to avoid farms, homes, or any areas where noise might present a problem to people on the ground.

In the first 20 hours of flight, the ultralight pilot should practice the ground reference maneuvers at wind speeds of less than 8-10 miles per hour. It takes a while to build the "seat-of-the-pants" sensing. During the first few hours of learning to fly, it is advisable to just "drive" around and get to know the airplane. The pilot can polish techniques later when he has developed a real "feel" for the craft. Again, this is advice from your author; *ask your flight instructor about this*. The instructor may want you to wait even longer before practicing *any* maneuver near the ground.

Ground Track Control

Because you are free of the ground, you will often be carried by the wind much like a hot air balloon. The comparison of a boat on a lake or a boat on a river also applies. You can see that a boat on a lake will more or less remain in place while a boat on a river may be carried for some distance. If the boat is moving across the river, from bank to bank, you can also see that the boat would have to make a correction upstream to simply go in a straight line. The same holds true for an aircraft moving in a wind. If a correction isn't made, the aircraft will drift wherever the wind takes it.

When flying in a straight line, the simplest method of staying on course with a crosswind is to *crab* the aircraft by turning slightly into the wind. It isn't difficult to see that without a drift correction, the aircraft would be 10 miles off course in one hour with a 10 mph wind blowing at your right or left wingtip. Just keep this fact in mind: If you have a wind blowing directly on either wingtip, in a one hour time period, you will be as far off course as the wind velocity is designated. If you want to study this further, there is a crosswind velocity chart in most FAA private and commercial study manuals that will give you the exact drift value. The important thing here is to develop the sense of needed correction for the wind in the environment during any particular flight.

One of the biggest problems student pilots

seem to have is determining the direction of the wind during a flight. Figure 4-18 shows some of the methods pilots use in determining the wind direction. One of the better ways, since lakes and ponds are everywhere, is to look at the flow of water. The lakes and ponds will show wind movement even in small breezes. Smoke rising from manufacturing plants or houses will also tell wind direction. Weathervanes and windmills are good but the wind has to be moving quite a bit for this to be reliable. Although sometimes unreliable, animals grazing will point their backsides to the wind. In winds above 5 knots, grain will appear to flow just like water, or a surf. Smoke or dust from nearby farm machinery will clearly show wind direction as well as clothes on clothes lines. Grass and weeds will bend away from the wind, and if you're low enough, you can observe it from the air.

What about the winds aloft? First, find yourself a straight line such as a fence row or a road. Simply fly down the row, or road, and notice the drift of the aircraft. It doesn't take long to determine the wind direction and the amount of correction you will have to make to fly a straight line (Fig. 4-19).

One of the best ways to practice wind correction is to make a series of S-turns using a road as a reference (Figs. 4-20, 4-21).

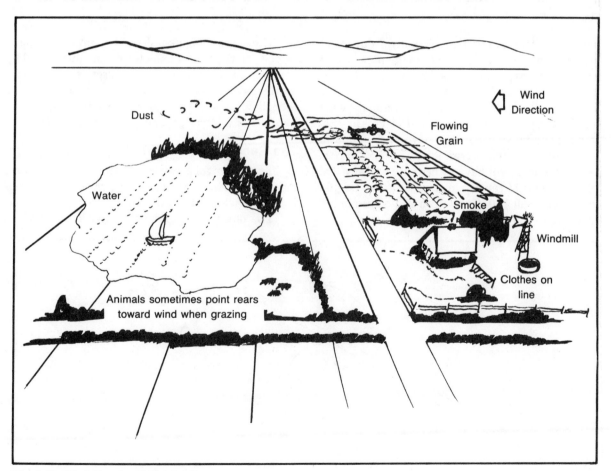

Fig. 4-18. Wind direction determinations.

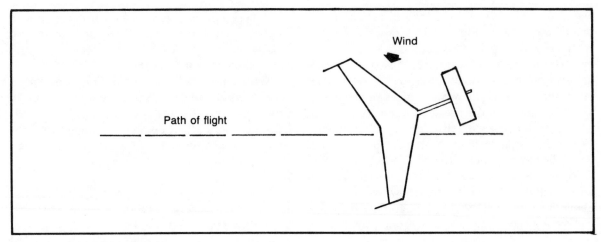

Fig. 4-19. Wind drift correction.

The pilot will enter the maneuver downwind and at right angles to the road. As the pilot crosses the road, a turn is made. The object will be to cross the road at the end of this 180 degree turn. At this point the pilot is now heading directly into the wind, or flying upwind. Immediately after crossing the road, the pilot starts another turn in the opposite direction. Since the aircraft is now heading into the wind, the turn will have to be more shallow than the first part of the S maneuver. Again, the pilot executes a full 180 degree turn and comes out 90 degrees to the road.

The degree of bank is dependent upon the wind velocity in the S-turn maneuver. The pilot should perform the steepest bank after crossing the road downwind because of the greatest ground speed. A shallow bank will be entered while flying upwind because of a lower ground speed (Fig. 4-22).

The Rectangular Pattern

The rectangular pattern or course is a practice maneuver flown so the ground track scribes a perfect rectangle on the ground.

The objective is to develop division of atten-

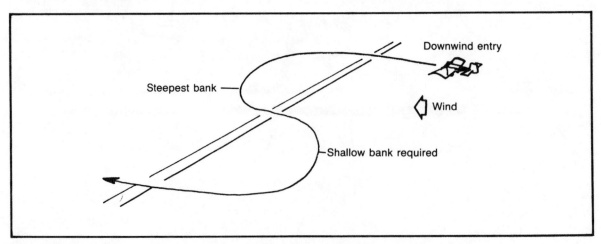

Fig. 4-20. S-turns across a road.

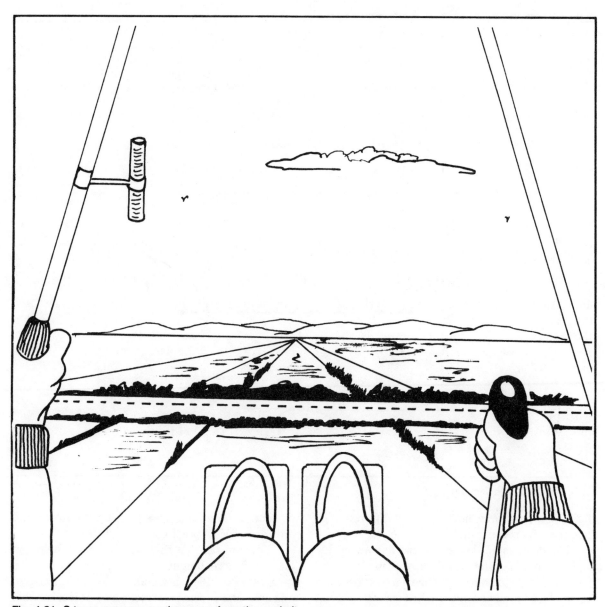

Fig. 4-21. S-turns across a road as seen from the cockpit.

tion between the flight path and the ground while controlling the aircraft. All of this is done while watching out for other aircraft! Another objective is to develop recognition of drift toward or away from a line parallel to the desired ground track (Fig. 4-23).

The Airport Traffic Pattern as Related to the Rectangular Pattern

To fly this maneuver, the pilot selects a rectangular area such as a field, approximately 1/4 to 1/2 mile on each side. The course is flown at an approximate altitude of 500 feet. Check this with your

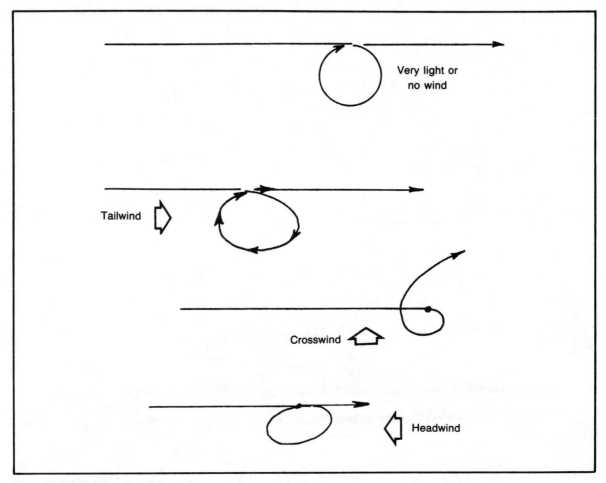

Fig. 4-22. Effect of a wind during a turn.

flight instructor first, however, as a different altitude may be recommended.

The entry is 45 degrees to the downwind leg of the area. The pilot will fly downwind until the first left turn is to be made. Then a new crosswind leg will be entered and again a drift correction must be made. In Fig. 4-24, you can see where a wind correction is made on each side of the rectangle.

After turning to and flying the first crosswind leg, the pilot will again make a left bank and enter the upwind portion. This leg is into the wind and if you have a crosswind component as you do in the Fig. 4-24, you will have to make the appropriate

correction. The final crosswind leg is entered and the rectangle is practiced to perfection.

You can see that this maneuver will help you learn to fly a rectangular traffic pattern. One of the greatest pilot killers is a stall in the traffic pattern, or a spin-entry from incorrect turns. It is advisable for you to learn to make the pattern turns at no more than 30 degrees of bank. A part of this maneuver is to also learn how to rollout on a precise heading as you would from base leg to final in the landing approach sequence (Figs. 4-24, 4-25).

If the pilot will work at perfecting this maneuver, it will be of great benefit when flying normal

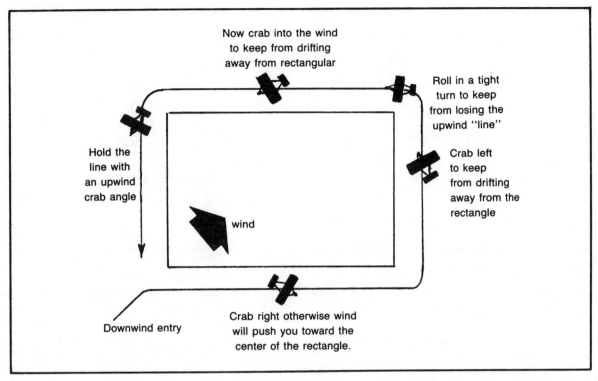

Fig. 4-23. The rectangular pattern.

traffic patterns. Stall and spin-entry accidents are far too common and most of them seem to occur because the pilot tried to make very steep turns at airspeeds too low for the traffic pattern.

THE IN-FLIGHT EMERGENCY

Before we prepare for a descent, let's take a closer look at the in-flight emergency and see how we can learn to deal with it. So it will be easier for

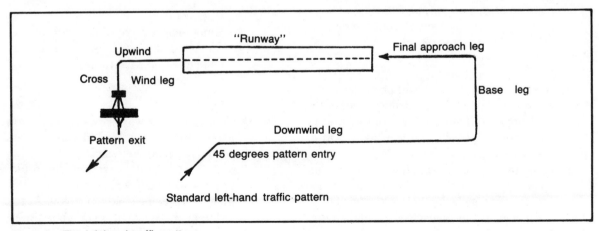

Fig. 4-24. The left-hand traffic pattern.

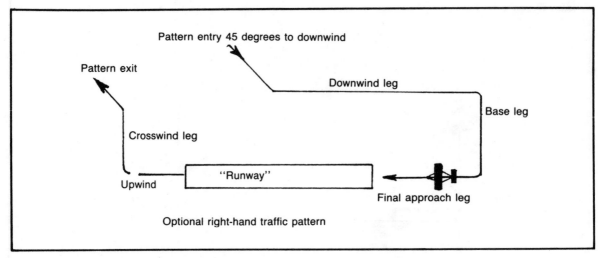

Fig. 4-25. The right-hand traffic pattern.

you to remember (memorize) the details, I am going to present this in a modified outline form.

A. The order of tasks in an emergency situation:
1. Aviate (Fly the thing).
2. Navigate (Find a suitable landing site).
3. Communicate (If possible, land close to civilization to get help).

B. Priorities
1. You
2. The airframe (If you have to break the airplane to save yourself, *do it*).
3. The engine (If you have to ruin the engine to save the airframe, *do it*).

C. Preventive Measures
1. Always fly high enough over obstacles to allow you to make a safe landing on an open area close by. If you fly over wooded areas, you must accept the risk of not having a safe place to land.
2. If you fly over underlying fog or clouds, you must accept the risk that if an engine failure occurs, you may be landing in zero visibility and could hit an obstacle in your landing path. Keep in mind that flying in these con-

ditions is prohibited by FAR 103.21.
3. Treat power lines, barbed wire, fences, and towers with healthy respect. If you must land over a power line, come in steep to clear them in the event you lose power altogether.

D. If you are involved in an accident away from home, think STOP:
1. **S**—Stay in the area.
2. **T**—Think about shelter.
3. **O**—Observe your personal condition:

    a. Physical condition.
    b. Emotional—are you in shock?
    c. Surroundings and how things may change if you have to stay for a while.
    d. Get organized.

4. **P** Plan. Always, always, always before you leave home on any kind of an extended flight, *tell someone* where you're going and when you plan to return. Let someone know that if you're not back by a given time, come looking for you. At the scene of the accident, plan what you're going to do until help arrives.

If the engine does fail, you should not panic; remember, the aircraft is a powered glider and a loss of power doesn't have to be a disaster. You can simulate a power loss by bringing the throttle back to near idle, and then pretend you have an engine failure. Keep in mind the two-stroke doesn't take kindly to prolonged idle periods. When that engine is cooling so rapidly on the outside, and is still hot in the combustion chamber, you're asking for a situation that may seize the engine if allowed to continue for a long time. If you are going to practice engine failure, be prepared for the real thing. Any time you try for a dead-stick situation, you may have just that!

Use the Boy Scout motto (Be Prepared) when you decide to simulate the engine-out. Look around below you and make sure that you can actually land the thing in case the engine *does* quit. If it does, "Aviate, navigate, then communicate!"

The very first thing you must do is fly the airplane. In case of engine failure, don't be looking around for "What happened?" Establish your best glide speed so the aircraft will descend without gaining airspeed. You should already know the best glide speed and that should be first order of business; look at the airspeed indicator and hold that glide speed with your pitch inputs. Once you're set on airspeed, look around for a suitable place to land. Note the wind so that your planning will put you landing into the wind. Providing you have enough time, try to set up some semblance of a traffic pattern. Again, *fly the airplane.*

Okay, you have the field the way you want and the airspeed is giving you a desired rate of descent. Now, see why it won't run. Again, keep in mind that the aircraft is first and foremost, always. If there is any doubt, get the bird safely on the ground, then try to fly it out of the pasture, or wherever you landed it.

If you have enough altitude to attempt a restart, your order of events should go something like this: (1) ignition switch; (2) throttle; (3) choke; (4) fuel check; then pull the cord to see if it starts. If not, go ahead and execute the approach and enjoy the glide.

If you want to try a dead-stick landing sometime, wait until you're on a final approach, the ground is within a wingspan's distance below you, and you have a good power off approach going for you; then simply switch off the ignition and glide in for a landing. This is about the safest way you can experience what it's like to make a "quiet" landing. Ask your flight instructor about this procedure. If he doesn't recommend that you try anything like this, then *don't*. You don't have to simulate any emergency, anytime. This is in case you absolutely feel it is the only way you can ever find out your limits. Safety first, then find your limits!

If the engine failure occurs during takeoff, *land straight ahead*. Many aircraft accidents have occurred because the pilot tried to make it back to the runway from which he just departed.

When the aircraft is climbing, the airspeed is low and if the pilot tries to make a steep turn, the stall speed may very well exceed the climb speed. If the wings are at a steep bank angle, and the rudder is deflected, the pilot may initiate or be near or in a *spin entry*. Your chances of walking away from a spin crash are very slim (Fig. 4-26). Most of these accidents are pointed straight down and guess who hits the ground first?

The question may come to mind about landing straight ahead; what if there are trees or powerlines ahead? Your chances of going between the trees or powerlines and making it are better than your chances of living through a spin-type crash.

The most undesirable type of emergency would be the mid-air collision. Nobody wins in this bout! However, if you are equipped with a parachute, you do have a chance of making it down. Assuming you have impacted and structure failure has occurred, the parachute is your only salvation. The parachutes are attached to the aircraft and it's up to you to rip open the pack and throw the chute. Some new "state-of-the-art" chutes have a charge that blows them clear of the aircraft and they deploy well above the problem (Fig. 4-27).

Fig. 4-26. A spin close to the ground with insufficient altitude for recovery.

DESCENT TO LANDING SEQUENCE

First and foremost, you must plan ahead before starting this final portion of your flight. If you have a game plan, it will help eliminate problems that can arise in the traffic pattern.

It is excellent piloting technique to overfly the landing area before starting the descent-to-landing sequence. If the airport of flight park has a segmented circle (Fig. 4-28) you can use this to check out the traffic pattern and inside the circle you'll find a windsock that will show the direction of the winds on the ground.

The recommended altitude for a fly-by is at least 400 feet AGL. Sailplane pilots have a "window" that they fly through that prepares them for

a landing sequence. This window is known as the *initial point*, or I.P.

Although I can't speak for your airport or flight park, I am recommending that you go through an I.P. in preparation for landing an ultralight. The pilot can start the descent to the downwing leg from the I.P. With an altitude of 400 feet AGL recom-

Fig. 4-27. Parachute recovery.

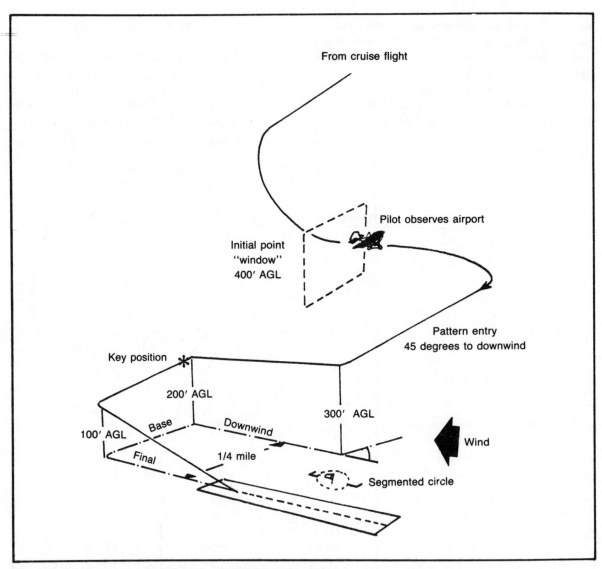

From cruise flight

Pilot observes airport

Initial point
"window"
400' AGL

Pattern entry
45 degrees to downwind

Key position

200' AGL

300' AGL

100' AGL

Base

Downwind

Wind

Final

1/4 mile

Segmented circle

Fig. 4-28. Descent to a landing sequence through the I.P. window.

mended for the I.P., the pilot should enter downwind at about 300 feet, turn base leg at 200 feet, and execute the final approach leg at 100 feet. These are easy numbers to remember and it helps keep the pilot organized when shooting the approach. Figure 4-28 shows the pattern entry at a 45 degrees angle and a turn to downwind at the recommended altitude of 300 feet. Note the pattern

is approximately 1/4 mile from the runway. This can vary and you should ask your instructor what is recommended in your local situation.

There is a point called the *key position* found at the beginning of the base leg (Fig. 4-29). This point is a good place to assess the approach to determine whether or not corrections are to be made. There are four factors that should be assessed: (1)

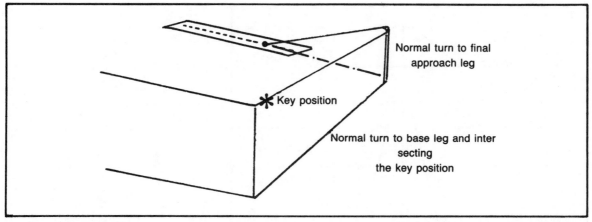

Fig. 4-29. The key position.

altitude; (2) airspeed; (3) winds; and (4) the distance from the runway. At the K.P., the pilot can either increase the airspeed or the altitude to compensate for winds and distances from the landing runway. Figure 4-30 shows how the pilot can make base and final leg corrections from the key position. If the aircraft is flying in erratic winds, it may be difficult to exactly judge where to make changes when on final approach. If the pilot will make adjustments at the key position, and do it correctly, the spot can be "nailed" time and time again. Throughout the approach, the pilot should monitor the aircraft's position and make any required adjustments to put the plane on the desired spot.

APPROACH

In any landing and in any type of aircraft the pilot should constantly be looking around for traffic. Again, be a "fighter pilot." You never know when some turkey will decide to cut you off and try to land ahead of you. Looking at the FARs, the

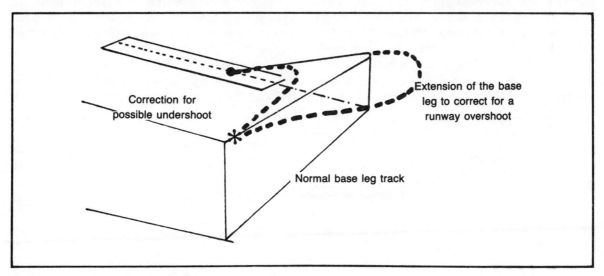

Fig. 4-30. Corrections after key position.

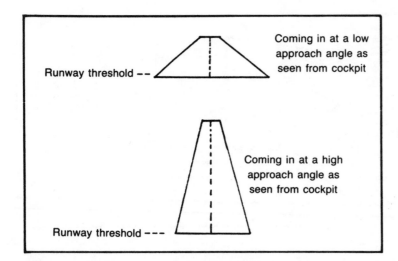

Fig. 4-31. Visual cues.

aircraft on final approach has the right-of-way over all other aircraft in the traffic pattern; however, this doesn't keep someone from taking that right-of-way (but all other types of aircraft have the right-of-way over ultralights).

The turn to final should be carefully planned and coordinated so that your rollout from the base leg should be on a runway centerline extension.

Throughout your approach, your ability to use references is important. Since your kinesthetic sensitivity is not fully developed at this stage of the game, you are going to have to use your vision references to program your mind and body.

One of the ways of programming your mind with visual cues is sizing up the shape of the runway. Figure 4-31 illustrates two visual cues showing how the shape of the runway will tell you if you're too high or too low in your approach.

The approach is a combination of controlling the airspeed and the attitude so that you will be able to put the airplane on the runway at exactly the desired spot. It is common for a beginning ultralight pilot to overcontrol the aircraft and make corrections that are unnecessary. Although your particular airplane may differ considerably, the average ultralight will make a final approach at about 35 miles per hour, diminishing to stall speed at touchdown. This is the most desirable type of approach, since you want the aircraft to transition from flight to taxi at a speed which is not going to put a strain on the landing gear.

If your approach altitude is too high, as shown in the lower half of Fig. 4-31, there is little value in diving the aircraft. The reason is the buildup of

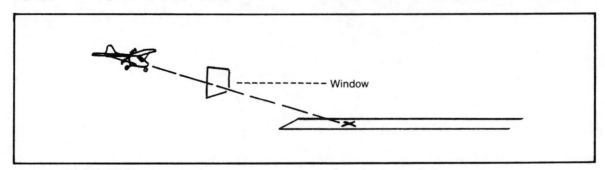

Fig. 4-32. Approach window.

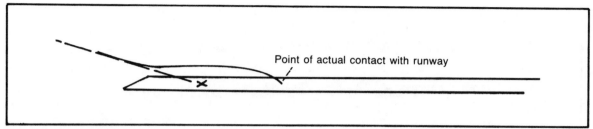

Point of actual contact with runway

Fig. 4-33. The flareout distance.

airspeed and subsequent tendency of the aircraft to float well beyond the desired landing spot. By the same measure, coming in too low may cause you to undershoot the runway. If there are obstructions, such as trees or powerlines, you may crash the aircraft by not having power or speed to get over them.

The approach speed is the same as the best angle-of-glide airspeed. Any airspeed above or below this will result in a greater rate of descent. It goes without saying that if the aircraft is going to undershoot the desired spot, the pilot *cannot stretch the glide* by raising the nose and slowing down. To get the aircraft on the desired line again, the power will have to be increased.

It is a good idea to discuss the descent profile with your flight instructor to find what is the recommended no-wind approach angle and airspeed. When you know the exact altitude, attitude, and airspeed, you can develop a window and fly through it every time you make your approach (Fig. 4-32). Such things as downdrafts, updrafts, wind shear, and crosswinds can be managed without having to worry about getting the right descent profile. Your body will have developed a kinesthetic sense that will take care of the "normal" for you. This is what they mean when they say you have developed a "seat-of-the-pants" flying technique. If you make your first habits dead perfect, when all the excitement comes, there will be far less tendency to make the wrong move.

The "spot" is the point where the glidepath and the runway intersect. However, your actual touchdown will occur down the runway after the flareout.

As the aircraft comes down the glide path, all objects beyond the "x" spot will appear to move away from the aircraft while objects closer will appear to move toward the aircraft. If you are doing it right, only the "x" will appear to be in the same relative position (Fig. 4-33).

The Flareout

At an altitude just above the ground, the pilot initiates a flareout by gradual increase in the back pressure on the control stick to reduce airspeed and decrease the rate of descent. It would be ideal for the aircraft to reach this point about one foot from the runway. The pilot would then hold that one foot of altitude as the aircraft slowly settles to the runway. This would be accomplished by pulling the control stick back until the critical angle of attack is achieved and the aircraft stalls just at touchdown.

The altitude where the pilot initiates the flare is determined by, again, visual clues. There is a proper focal point (Fig. 4-34) where the pilot focuses at flareout. If the pilot focuses too close to the craft, the speed will blur objects on the ground and this may cause the pilot to react by overcontrolling. If the pilot focuses too far down the runway, things will seem to go on in slow-motion and reactions in this phase will be delayed, causing the pilot to undercontrol. It might happen that the pilot would literally "fly into the ground" and a subsequent bounce might throw the craft into the air at speeds very near stall. This could lead to a series of events that may result in a crash. The whole idea is to find a point that is neither too close nor too far from the nose of the aircraft.

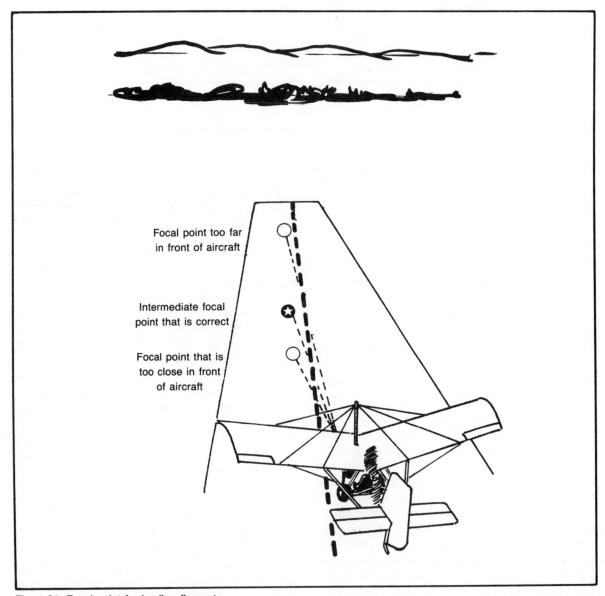

Fig. 4-34. Focal point for landing flareout.

The Way It Looks from the Cockpit

See Fig. 4-35. You are now on final approach to land. You can see the desired landing spot which is at the end of your flight path. All objects above the spot will tend to move away from you and all closer to you, from this spot, will tend to move under you as you make your approach.

See Fig. 4-36. You notice the spot is not moving. It stays right where you want it. Airspeed should be about 25 to 30 miles per hour at this point and you should have picked your flareout focus point.

See Fig. 4-37. The focus point is determined and the airspeed is diminishing as the pilot begins to stop the rate of descent by increasing the pitch.

The airspeed is decreasing to near stall and the power is brought back to idle.

See Fig. 4-38. The pilot tries to hold one foot

Fig. 4-35. On final approach at 100 feet altitude.

Fig. 4-36. On final approach at 25 feet altitude.

of altitude by back pressure on the control stick. When the aircraft reaches stall speed, it will settle gently to the earth.

THE CROSSWIND LANDING

Most of the time ultralight pilots won't have to worry about the crosswind landing since the ultralight can land in a very small area and all the pilot has to do is point it into the wind and land straight ahead. That is one of the absolute joys of this kind of flying.

However, the time will come when you have to contend with the situation and it's best you know the basics.

A crosswind landing can be very tricky, espe-

Fig. 4-37. On final approach, 5 feet altitude, 10 feet from touchdown.

Fig. 4-38. Touchdown with pitch-up attitude to flare the aircraft.

cially if the winds are above 10 knots. Just remember, the air mass is moving and so is the aircraft; the ground, however is not moving and therein lies the problem. That runway is going to stay right where they put it; you are going to have to maneuver your craft in a moving environment so that it makes contact at exactly the right point and stays where you put it!

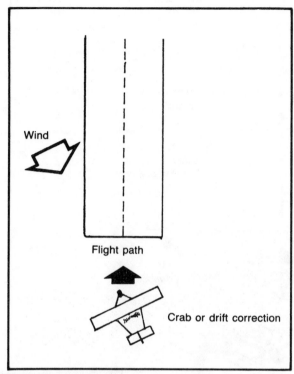

Fig. 4-39. Drift correction.

Let's start with the wind directly in front of you. There is no big problem, since the craft usually doesn't want to go sideways and since the headwind reduces your groundspeed, your landing roll will be shorter. Now, move the wind 45 degrees to your left and imagine it is blowing around 8 knots. A component of that wind is trying to move you off course and another component is trying to slow you down. The pilot must make a *drift correction* to keep the wind from blowing the aircraft off the runway. The stronger the crosswind, the greater the correction that must be made (Fig. 4-39).

The wind that is 90 degrees to the nose of the aircraft, or just off either wingtip, requires some special consideration. The closer the wind is to the 90 degrees, or perpendicular, the greater the required wind correction angle. The approach airspeed also has a lot to do with the crab angle. The slower the airspeed, the greater the crab angle; conversely, the greater the airspeed, the less the crab angle.

Sometimes pilots slip the aircraft when approaching in a crosswind. A slip is performed by lowering one wing (as you would into the wind) and using opposite rudder to maintain the desired direction. It should be noted that this technique does not work well with spoilerons. It is mainly an aileron maneuver (Fig. 4-40).

TOUCHDOWN

Once the aircraft nears the ground, in a slip, the pilot must transition from the slip to touchdown without the wind moving the aircraft sideways. The aircraft cannot be landed sideways without putting a load on the landing gear. Due to the crosswind, the aircraft will want to weathervane the moment you straighten it out. The pilot should keep the aileron on the upwind side up and the downwind aileron down to keep the aircraft in correct alignment. The rudder should be turned *away from* the wind. All of this correction keeps the wind from lifting the upwind wing and the rudder action keeps the craft from weathervaning (Fig. 4-41).

And finally, if you think you're not making the whole crosswind maneuver correctly, *go around*. It's not bad pilot technique to admit you've done it wrong. Any knowledgeable pilot on the ground will admire you for the fact that you're using your head. The most embarrassing thing is to go ahead and execute the approach and then bend the bird.

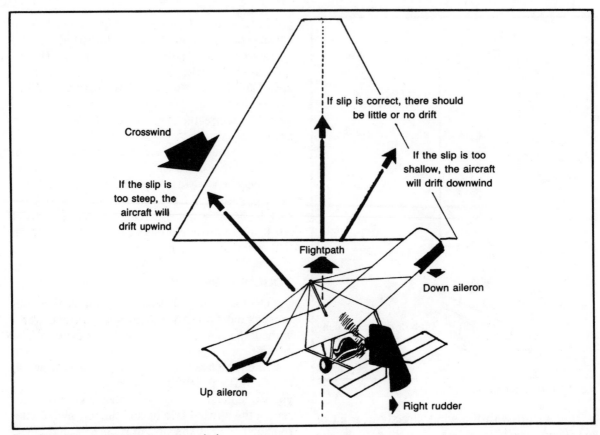

Fig. 4-40. Slip to a landing in a crosswind.

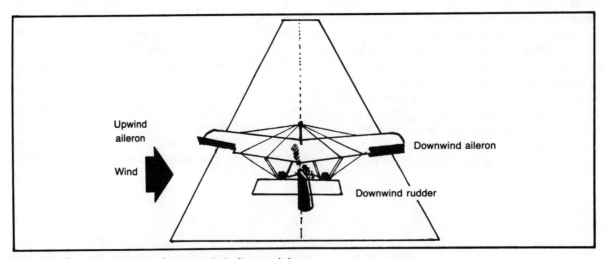

Fig. 4-41. Ground corrections for crosswind after touchdown.

Chapter 5

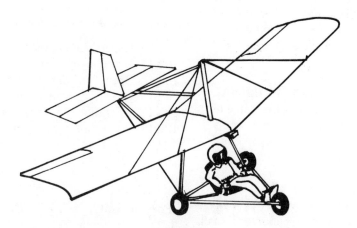

The Ultralight Pilot and the Law

Most everyone is overjoyed by the fact the FAA is not requiring ultralight aircraft to be licensed, or the pilots to be certificated. However, we must realize that flying an unlicensed aircraft still requires responsibility to *all* other aircraft in the airspace.

There have been problems. In isolated instances, ultralight pilots have been known to totally disregard the rights of others, creating a mid-air collision hazard with other aircraft. These individuals must be stopped if the sport is to thrive in an element of freedom. It is the responsibility of every pilot to bring pressure against those individuals that are giving ultralight flying a bad name. If we don't bring pressure against these outlaws, the FAA will step in and do it for us.

LOCAL LAWS

Most states now have statutes governing hang gliders, ultralights, and balloons. These laws are often very specific in their limitation and the pilot should check the statutes before taking flight. Even if your state doesn't have the law spelled out for

ultralight flight, you may very well be subject to two fundamental regulations that exist in all states. Using Colorado as an example, let me show you what I mean.

In the State of Colorado, an ultralight pilot can get into trouble for two specific reasons. First, there is the law of *nuisance*. Here's how the statute reads:

18-9-106 DISORDERLY CONDUCT. A person commits disorderly conduct if he intentionally, knowingly, or recklessly: (c) . . . makes unreasonable noise in a public place or near a private residence that he has no right to occupy.

In the State of Colorado, violation of this law is a Class-One petty offense and is punishable by a maximum fine of $500 and six months confinement.

Secondly, you can get arrested for *criminal trespass*. This statute reads:

18-4-503. SECOND DEGREE CRIMINAL

TRESPASS. A person commits the crime of second degree criminal trespass if he unlawfully enters or remains in or upon premises which are enclosed in a manner designed to exclude intruders or fenced. Second degree criminal trespass is a Class-Three misdemeanor.

18-4-504. THIRD DEGREE CRIMINAL TRESPASS. A person commits the crime of third degree criminal trespass if he unlawfully enters or remains in or upon premises. Third degree criminal trespass is a Class-One petty offense.

A Class-Three misdemeanor carries a maximum of $750 fine, with up to six months in jail.

If you are flying too low, even away from FAA-controlled airspace, too close to persons or property, you can see from the above how you might be considered a nuisance. If you land away from an airport, on private property, you could be arrested for trespassing. A good rule of thumb is to stay at least 500 feet away from anyone and his property, and avoid landing on private property.

FEDERAL AVIATION REGULATIONS

As of September 2, 1982, the Federal Aviation Administration made an official ruling on ultralight aircraft. This new regulation is known as Part 103.

The Director of Emery School of Aviation once gave me this advice: "When it comes to FARs, don't paraphrase; quote the law exactly as it states." This is sound advice, since the pilot is responsible to *know the law*, and often when someone says ". . . in other words," they can mislead the other person. So, here is the new Part 103 as it was printed in the *Federal Register*, Volume 47, Number 171.

Part 103—ULTRALIGHT VEHICLES

Subpart A—General
Sec.
103.1 Applicability.

103.3 Inspection requirements.
103.5 Waivers.
103.7 Certification and registration.

Subpart B—Operating Rules.

103.9 Hazardous operations.
103.11 Daylight operations.
103.13 Operation near aircraft; right of way rules.
103.15 Operation over congested areas.
103.17 Operations in certain airspace.
103.19 Operations in prohibited or restricted areas.
103.21 Visual reference to the surface.
103.23 Flight visibility and cloud clearance requirements.

(For Authority, see *Federal Register*, Vol. 47, no. 171)

103.1 Applicability.

This part prescribes rules governing the operation of ultralight vehicles in the U.S. For the purposes of this part, an ultralight vehicle is a vehicle that:

(a) Is used or intended to be used for manned operation in the air by a single occupant;
(b) Is used or intended to be used for recreation or sport purposes only;
(c) Does not have any U.S. or foreign airworthiness certificate;
and
(d) If unpowered, weighs less than 155 pounds; or
(e) If powered:

   (1) Weighs less than 254 pounds empty weight, excluding floats and safety devices which are intended for deployment in a potentially catastrophic situation;
   (2) Has a fuel capacity not exceeding 5 U.S. gallons; (30 pounds)
   (3) Is not capable of more than 55 knots (63.25 mph statute) calibrated airspeed at full power in level flight; and
   (4) Has a power-off stall speed which does not

exceed 24 knots (27.6 miles per hour statute) calibrated airspeed.

AUTHOR'S NOTE—Calibrated airspeed is defined as "Indicated airspeed of an aircraft, corrected for position and instrument error. Calibrated airspeed is equal to true airspeed in a standard atmosphere at sea level."

103.3 Inspection requirements

(a) Any person operating an ultralight vehicle under this part shall, upon request, allow the Administrator (FAA), or his designee, to inspect the vehicle to determine the applicability of this part.
(b) The pilot or operator of an ultralight vehicle must, upon request of the Administrator, furnish satisfactory evidence that the vehicle is subject only to the provision of this part.

103.5 Waivers.

No person may conduct operations that require a deviation from this part except under a written waiver issued by the Administrator.

103.7 Certification and registration.

(a) Notwithstanding any other section pertaining to certification of aircraft or other parts or equipment, ultralight vehicles and their component parts and equipment are not required to meet the airworthiness certification standards specified for aircraft or to have certificates of airworthiness.
(b) Notwithstanding any other section pertaining to airman certification, *Operators of ultralight vehicles* are not required to meet any aeronautical knowledge, age, or experience requirements to operate those vehicles or to have airman or medical certificates.
(c) Notwithstanding any other section pertaining to registration and marking of aircraft,

ultralight vehicles are not required to be registered or to bearmarkings of any type.

SUBPART B—OPERATING RULES

103.9 Hazardous operations.

(a) No person may operate any ultralight vehicle in a manner that creates a hazard to other persons or property.
(b) No person may allow an object to be dropped from an ultralight vehicle if such action creates a hazard to other persons or property.

103.11 Daylight operations.

(a) No person may operate an ultralight vehicle except between the hours of sunrise and sunset.
(b) Notwithstanding paragraph (a) of this section, ultralight vehicles may be operated during the twilight periods 30 minutes before official sunrise and 30 minutes after official sunset or, in Alaska, during the period of civil twilight as defined in the Air Almanac if:

(1) The vehicle is equipped with an operating anticollision light visible for at least 3 statute miles; and
(2) All operations are conducted in uncontrolled airspace.

103.13 Operation near aircraft; Right-of-way rules.

(a) Each person operating an ultralight vehicle shall maintain vigilance so as to see and a void aircraft and shall yield the right-of-way to all aircraft.
(b) No person may operate an ultralight vehicle in a manner that creates a collision hazard with respect to aircraft.
(c) Powered ultralight shall yield the right-of-way to unpowered ultralights.

103.15 Operations over congested areas.

No person may operate an ultralight vehicle over any congested area of a city, town, or settlement, or over any open air assembly of persons.

103.17 Operations in certain airspace.

No person may operate an ultralight vehicle within an airport traffic area (Fig. 5-1), control zone, terminal control area, or positive control area unless that person has prior authorization from the air traffic control facility having jurisdiction over that airspace.

103.19 Operations in prohibited or restricted areas.

No person may operate an ultralight vehicle in prohibited or restricted areas unless that person has permission from the using or controlling agency, as appropriate.

103.21 Visual reference with the surface.

No person may operate an ultralight vehicle except by visual reference with the surface.

103.23 Flight visibility and cloud clearance requirements.

No person may operate an ultralight vehicle when the flight visibility or distance from clouds is less than that in the following table (Table 5-1); as appropriate:

FEDERAL REGULATIONS INDIRECTLY APPLICABLE TO ULTRALIGHTS

If we really want to impress the FAA and prove that we're trying to do things right, let's go their new Part 103 one better and learn some other regulations that may be of value to ultralighting.

Other Parts of the FARs may help the beginner understand the overall workings of the controlled and uncontrolled airspace. Part 1 covers General Definitions. Take a look at these and maybe it will answer some questions.

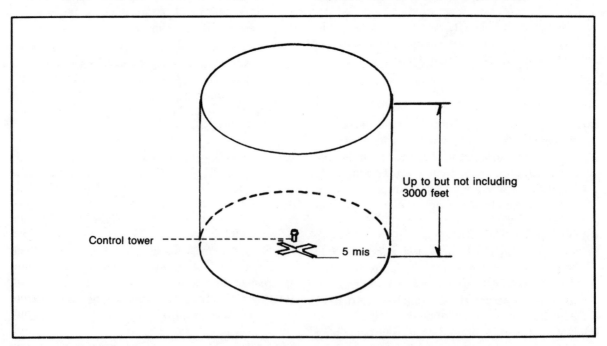

Fig. 5-1. Airport traffic area.

Table 5-1. Flight Visibility and Cloud Clearance Minimums.

Flight Altitudes	Vis. Min.	Minimum Distance From Clouds
1,200 feet or less above the surface regardless of MSL* altitude:		
(1) Within controlled airspace.	3	500 feet below, 1,000 feet above, 2,000 feet horizontal.
(2) Outside controlled airspace.	1	Clear of Clouds.
More than 1,200 feet above the surface but less than 10,000 feet MSL.*		
(1) Within controlled airspace.	3	500 feet below, 1,000 feet above, 2,000 feet horizontal.
(2) Outside controlled airspace.	1	500 feet below, 1,000 feet above, 2,000 feet horizontal.
More than 1,200 feet above the surface and at or above 10,000 feet MSL.*	5	1,000 feet below, 1,000 feet above, 1 statute mile horizontal.

*MSL—above Mean (average) Sea Level

1.1 General Definitions

"Airplane" means an engine-driven fixed-wing aircraft heavier than air, that is supported in flight by the dynamic reaction of the air against its wings. "Airport" is an area that is used for landing and takeoff of aircraft and includes its buildings and facilities, if any.

"Airport Traffic Area" (Let me explain this one for you: The ATA is an FAA designated airspace around airports having a control tower. For the ultralight pilot, this is restricted airspace. The ATA goes out 5 statute (regular) miles from the geographical center of the airport to the edge. The ATA extends up to, but not including 3000 feet above ground level. One thing I would like to point out here is sometimes confusing to ground school participants. This is the difference between a *Control Zone* and an *ATA*: A control zone differs from an ATA because of weather restrictions. A control zone is restrictive only when conditions get worse than the minimums. Since you are going to be flying visual, it stands to reason that you don't want to fly in an airport when all of the traffic is instrument regulated. For the sake of simplicity, just avoid control zones and ATAs).

"Ceiling" means the height above the earth's surface of the lowest layer of clouds or obscuring phenomena that is reported as broken, overcast, or obscured, and not classified as thin or partial.

"Controlled Airspace" means airspace designated as a continental control area, control area, control zone, terminal control area, or transition area, within which some or all aircraft may be subject to air traffic control.

"Visibility" means the average forward horizontal distance, from the cockpit of an aircraft in flight, at which prominent unlighted objects may be seen and identified by day.

"Prohibited Area" means airspace within which flight of aircraft is wholly prohibited.

"Restricted Area" means airspace . . . within which the flight of aircraft, while not wholly prohibited, is subject to restriction.

"VFR": visual flight rules.

"IFR": instrument flight rules.

"Traffic Pattern" means the flow of traffic that is prescribed for aircraft landing at, taxiing on, or taking off from, an airport.

FAR Part 91 is a set of operating rules for general aviation pilots. Although the ultralight pilot is not bound by this set of rules, it is good to know the rules of the licensed pilots and to know the operating limitations of general aviation aircraft. Some of these rules should be used as a guideline by the ultralight pilot.

91.3 The pilot in command of an aircraft is directly responsible for, and is the final AUTHORITY as to the operation of that aircraft.

91.5 (This reg covers preflight action that every pilot should check before a flight): . . . before beginning a flight, familiarize himself with all available information concerning that flight. This information must include: (a) for a flight not in the vicinity of an airport, weather reports and forecasts,

fuel requirements, and alternatives available if the planned flight cannot be completed. For any flight, runway lengths at airports of intended use, and the . . . landing and takeoff distance information.

91.9 No person may operate an aircraft in a careless or reckless manner so as to endanger the life or property of another.

91.11 (This regulation covers the liquor and drug use. Just remember, "eight hours between bottle and throttle.")

91.65 No person may operate an aircraft so close to another aircraft as to create a collision hazard. No person may operate an aircraft in formation flight except by arrangement with the pilot of each aircraft in formation . . .

91.67 (I was surprised the FAA didn't include this in the new Part 103. However, since they didn't, let's put it in our text so you'll know. This regulation is known as Right of Way Rules.) When a rule of this section gives another aircraft the right of way, he shall give way to that aircraft and may not pass over, under, or ahead of it, unless well clear . . . An aircraft in distress has the right of way over all other aircraft . . . When aircraft of the same category are converging at approximately the same altitude (with the exception of head-on), the aircraft to the other's right has the right of way. If the aircraft are of different categories:

(1) A balloon has the right of way over any category;
(2) A glider has the right of way over an airship, airplane or rotorcraft.
(3) An airship has the right of way over an airplane or rotorcraft.

However, an aircraft towing or refueling another aircraft has the right of way over all other engine-driven aircraft. (It might be of interest to note that a powered ultralight is at the very bottom of the right-of-way list.)

When approaching head-on, each pilot of each aircraft shall alter course to the right to pass

Table 5-2. Tower Light Signals.

Color and Type	Aircraft/Surface	Aircraft/Flight
Steady Green	Cleared for Takeoff	Cleared to Land
Flashing Green	Cleared to Taxi	Return For Landing
Steady Red	Stop	Give Way To Others
Flashing Red	Taxi Clear of Runway	Airport Unsafe—Don't Land
Flashing White	Return to Starting Point on the Airport	Not Applicable
Alternate Red And Green	Exercise Extreme Caution	Exercise Extreme Caution

well clear. When overtaking, the pilot of the overtaking aircraft shall alter his course to the right to pass well clear.

Aircraft while on final approach to land, or while landing, have the right of way over all other aircraft in flight or operating on the surface. When two or ore aircraft are approaching an airport for the purpose of landing, the aircraft at the lower altitude has the right of way, but it shall not take advantage of this rule to cut in front of another craft which is on final approach to land, or to overtake that aircraft.

Sometimes it may be necessary to go into a controlled airport to get parts or whatever. You must first contact the tower, usually by phone, before entering the Airport Traffic Area. The tower will have lights to guide you since you are not radioequipped, and Table 5-2 shows the light signals officially used by the FAA towers.

Chapter 6

Airspace Limitations

The standard map for VFR flight used by general aviation is the "Sectional." The Sectional map is quite easy to learn and will be a valuable aid to the ultralight pilot. In Fig. 6-1, you will see what the various symbols are that are used on the map.

THE SECTIONAL MAP

Using the example in Fig. 6-1, see if you can find, from Fig. 6-2, the symbol for an uncontrolled airport. The airport shown is "Alexander" and the information about that airport is shown about 3/8ths inch above and to the right. The field elevation is 7489, and the airport has a beacon (the small star above the symbol). This airport serves the town of Salida and has a hard surface runway 6000 feet long ("60"). The runways are lighted as shown by the capital "L" between the 7489 and the 60. The "122.8" is the frequency of the advisory service that is available. This service is called a "Unicom."

The lower portion of the legend (Fig. 6-3) covers "Airport Traffic Service and Airspace Information." This part is especially important to the

ultralight pilot since it shows what areas are to be *avoided*. Take for instance the Airport Traffic Area: The ATA is an area that you are not allowed to go in to without two-way radio contact with the tower. Just remember, when you violate controlled airspace, you are subject to FAA law. The areas to be avoided are emphasized by black arrows.

Since you are going to be flying at relatively low altitudes, I have pointed out, using the "lined" arrows, the obstructions. It has already happened; an ultralight pilot flew into the guy wires of a huge tower officially known as an obstruction. Know where these are and avoid them like the plague! Study the sectional and plan your flights away from restricted airspace and all obstructions.

CONTROLLED AIRSPACE

Previously I mentioned the Airport Traffic Area (ATA). Although the ATA is not shown on a sectional map, it is assumed if the airport has a federally operated tower. The ATA goes out 5 statute miles from the center of the airport and extends

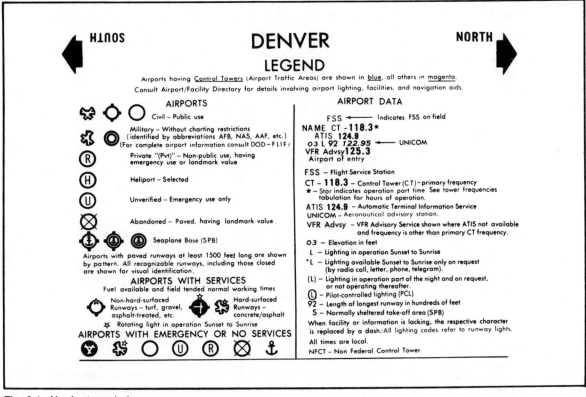

Fig. 6-1. Air chart symbols.

up to, but not including, 3000 feet above the surface. As an ultralight pilot, these are strictly prohibited unless you have prior permission for entry. These are not to be confused with control zones. The ATA is for control of air traffic.

The Airport Traffic Area

Figure 6-4 shows what a controlled airport looks like on the sectional map. Airports with towers are colored blue. Sometimes the control zone and the ATA are confused. Notice the "dashed" line around the airport. This is a control zone. The ATA is *not* illustrated.

The Weather Minimums For VFR Flight

To understand controlled airspace, you must first know that weather minimums and controlled

airspace are closely related. When conditions get worse than shown in Table 6-1, VFR flight is illegal. The FAA has very strict limitations on the available airspace and it is up to you to learn where you can legally fly.

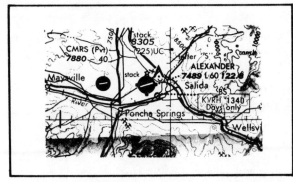

Fig. 6-2. Uncontrolled airport as shown on a Sectional chart.

Table 6-1. VFR Weather Minimums.

Altitude	Flight Visibility	Distance From Clouds
0-1200 feet above the surface		
In controlled airspace	3 statute miles	500 feet below 1000 feet above 2000 feet horizontal
Outside of controlled airspace	1 statute mile	Clear of clouds
1200-10,000 above the surface		
In controlled airspace	3 statute miles	500 feet below 1000 feet above 2000 feet horizontal
Outside of controlled airspace	1 statute mile	500 feet below 1000 feet above 2000 feet horizontal

The Control Zone

FAR Part 103 prohibits flight into *any* control zone. Shown in Fig. 6-5 is a control zone surrounding Durango (Colorado) airport. There are what is known as Transition Areas surrounding some control zones and they are color coded blue and magenta. It would be a good idea for you to get a current Sectional of your area and seek out the control zones. The control zone shown in Fig. 6-5 is bordered by a dashed line.

Terminal Control Area, TRSAs and Small Control Zones

The TCA looks like an upside-down wedding cake. If you look at the Denver TCA, notice Stapleton International Airport first (Fig. 6-6). This is the center and, on a wedding cake, that would be where the little figurines are located. Now, note the first layer; this is bounded by the heavy line. The other layers branch out from the first layer, etc. Let's say you wanted to land at Centennial Airport (South of Stapleton) and, by calling ahead to get clearance to land with light signals, you are now wondering if it is legal to enter the proximity as shown. The answer is yes—note the floor around Arapahoe starts at 8000 feet. This is shown by the "110/80" just below and to the left of the airport symbol. This means that as long as you don't go above 8000, you can go under the "layer" and fly on into Centennial Airport. The "bottom line" is this: They don't want you flying VFR into a TCA for *any* reason. It is a high-density traffic area and the aircraft that fly into the TCA are usually high-performance. For the ultralight, a good rule of thumb is *avoid the TCA at the blue line edge*. One thing I failed to mention was the possibility of wake turbulence when flying in or near a TCA.

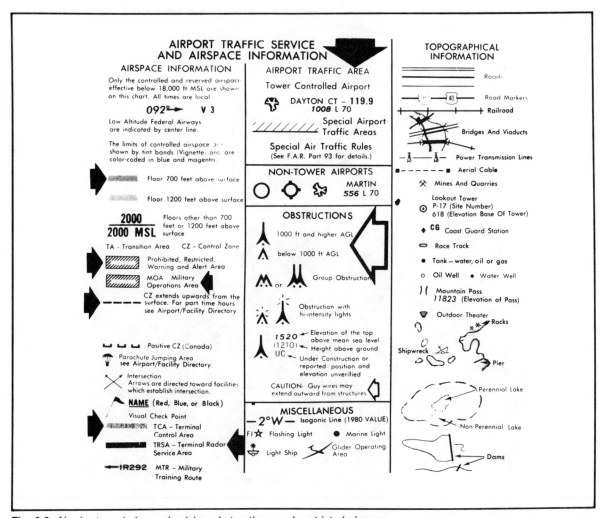

Fig. 6-3. Air chart symbols emphasizing obstructions and restricted airspace.

Like the TCA, the TRSA is an area of relatively high density aircraft traffic (Fig. 6-7). Colorado Springs is not as big as Denver but they do have a lot of military and airline traffic into and out of the airport. It is therefore suggested that you avoid the red line as much as possible.

The control zones mentioned previously were often associated with large airports. Figure 6-8 shows an example of a control zone surrounding a small airport. Again, control zones are weather-related.

ALERT AREAS AND THE MOAs

MOAs are for the very high performance, high-speed military aircraft at low altitude. Note they begin at 1500 feet and go up to 13,000 feet in the example in Fig. 6-9. You run the risk of wake turbulence and possible mid-air collisions when you cross these corridors!

Although Alert Areas (Fig. 6-10) are not prohibited, you must take caution when flying near them. Keep your eyes open for high performance

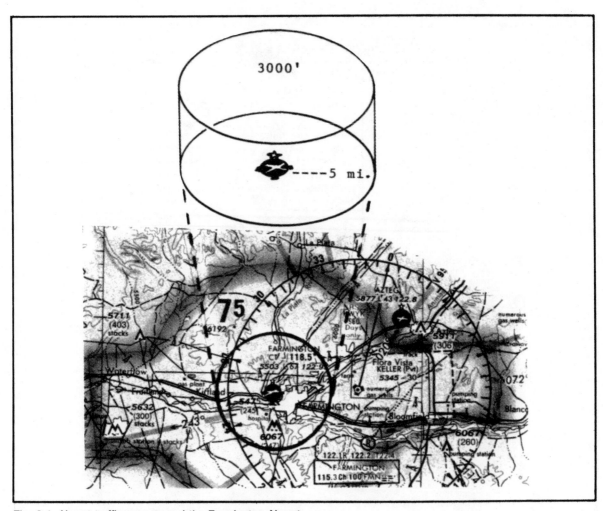

Fig. 6-4. Airport traffic area around the Farmington Airport.

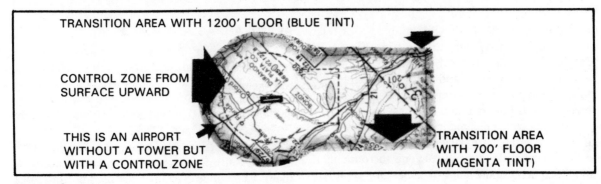

Fig. 6-5. Control zone.

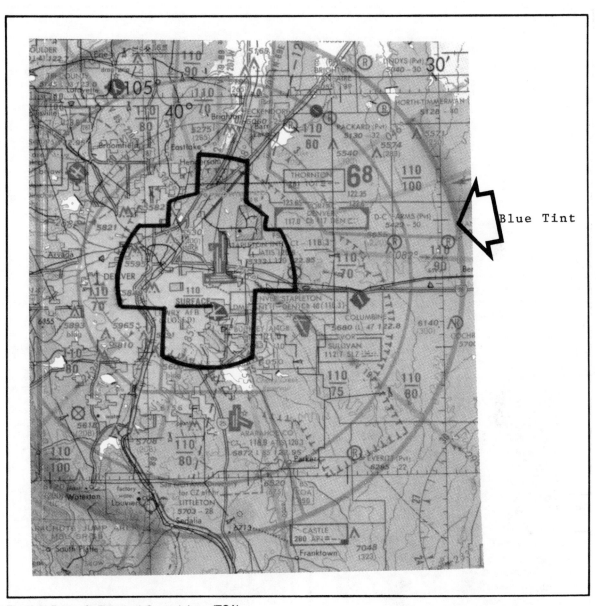

Blue Tint

Fig. 6-6. Denver's Terminal Control Area (TCA).

aircraft or other hazards to your flight. It would be wise just to avoid this situation.

SPECIAL AREAS TO AVOID

Sometimes certain areas are to be avoided for reasons other than airspace regulations. The wilderness area is an example of one you should avoid (Fig. 6-11). The government looks with disfavor upon pilots who disturb the birdies—especially with noisy ultralights! If your flight is going to cross a

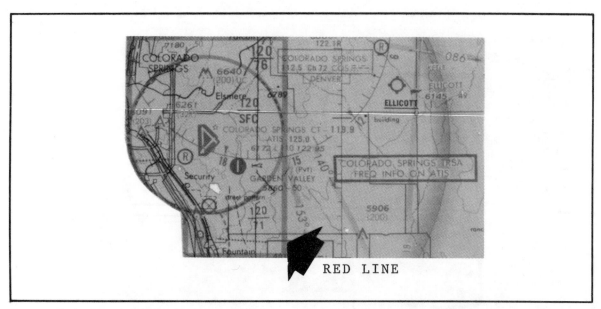

Fig. 6-7. Typical Terminal Radar Service Area (TRSA).

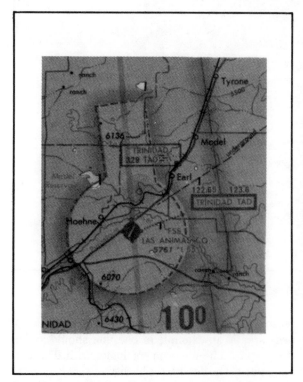

Fig. 6-8. A typical Control Zone at a small airport.

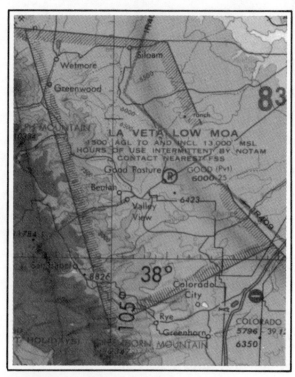

Fig. 6-9. Military Operations Area.

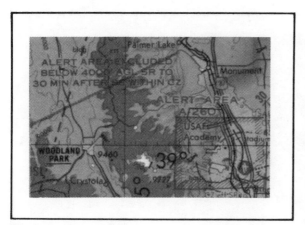

Fig. 6-10. Alert Areas.

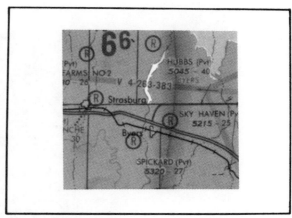

Fig. 6-12. Restricted Airports.

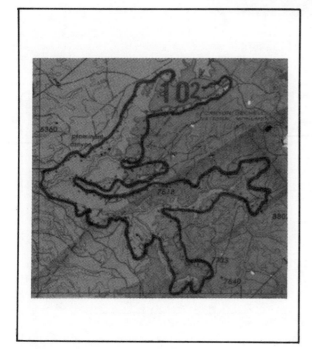

Fig. 6-11. Wilderness Area.

wilderness area, it is wise to go around it—not only for the birdies, but if you happen to lose an engine in the area, it might take a while to find you!

Note all of the Rs in the round circles in Fig. 6-12. These are restricted airports. The person, or company, that owns the airport doesn't want the public landing on this property. If you happen to be flying along and see an airstrip that looks like a friendly place to land, you might not get a warm welcome if you go in for a visit. Avoid restricted private airports.

RESTRICTED OR PROHIBITED AREAS

Certain areas are restricted and flying into these require permission from the governing authority. Please note that we have a restricted area in Fig. 6-13 and I have shown you how to find the governing authority. These areas are set aside for a reason, and you should take every precaution to avoid flying through the area unless you have contacted the controlling authority and have received permission to enter.

PROHIBITED, RESTRICTED, WARNING, AND ALERT AREAS
ON DENVER SECTIONAL CHART

NO.	NAME	ALTITUDE	TIME	APPROPRIATE AUTHORITY
P-26	Denver, Colo.	To 6900	Continuous	C.O., Rocky Mountain Arsenal, Denver, Colo.
R-2601	Fort Carson, Colo.	To 35,000	Continuous	† FAA, Denver ARTC Center, Area FSS. C.G. Fort Carson, Colo.
R-2602	Fort Carson, Colo.	To 35,000	Continuous	† FAA, Denver ARTC Center Area FSS. C.G. Fort Carson, Colo.
R-5101	Los Alamos, New Mexico	To 12,000	Continuous	Mgr., Energy Research & Development Administration, Los Alamos, N. Mex.
R-6410	Blanding, Utah	Unlimited	By NOTAM 12 hr in advance.	† FAA, Denver ARTC Center Area FSS. Deputy AF, Armament Development & Testing Center, White Sands Missile Range, New Mexico
R-6413	Green River, Utah	Unlimited	By NOTAM 48 hr in advance.	† FAA, Denver ARTC Center Area FSS. Deputy for Air Force, White Sands Missile Range, New Mexico 88002
A-260	Colorado Springs, Colo.	To 17,500	Daily SR-SS	

P - Prohibited   R - Restricted   W - Warning   A - Alert   † - Controlling Agency   ˙ - For Information Only
Unless otherwise noted: Altitudes are MSL and in feet; time is local.
No person shall operate an aircraft within a Prohibited Area, or within a Restricted Area between the designated
   altitudes during the time of designation unless prior permission has been issued by the appropriate authority as
   listed above. The appropriate authority is defined as either the controlling agency (†) or the using agency.
Flight within Alert Areas is not restricted, but pilots are advised to exercise extreme caution.

Fig. 6-13. Prohibited, Restricted, Warning, and Alert Areas.

Chapter 7

Meteorology

I overheard a flight instructor talking to a group about who makes the best ultralight pilot. I think you might be interested to know what was said: "I have flown with at least 50 students now, and I have come to the conclusion that someone without previous aeronautical training makes a better pilot than someone who has a general aviation background!" Someone in the group asked the inevitable question: "Why?"

He continued: "Well, a pilot with previous training doesn't take the wind as seriously as a non-pilot. The trained pilot isn't really concerned about wind conditions until things start blowing around 20 knots. The wind sock has to be standing straight out before it gets his attention!"

Whether this is true or not I couldn't say; I only know that one basic fact was brought to light in their discussion. The wind is a *major* factor in ultralight flying and when you ask yourself what is important, wind must be very high on the meteorological priority list.

THE REALM OF FLIGHT

Considering the weather realms that we fly in, an interesting progression can be observed from the ultralight to the airliner. Consider the altitudes:

- ☐ 0—1000' AGL (Above Ground Level): Ultralights/hangliders.
- ☐ 1000—5000' AGL: Recreational general aviation.
- ☐ 1000-10,000' AGL: Serious VFR and IFR general aviation.
- ☐ 10,000—25,000' AGL: IFR and high-performance general aviation.
- ☐ 25,000' up: Commercial, corporate, and military.

It is a fact that a turbine engine operates most efficiently at very high altitudes; however, it is not so well known that most weather occurs *below* 18,000 feet. This is why it is so comfortable on most airline flights when you are cruising along at 33,000 feet; all the weather is below you.

Unfortunately, the ultralight and general aviation pilot has to contend with the weather and all of its constantly changing characteristics. Since our "realm" of flight is mostly below 1000 feet AGL, we will concentrate on the weather within that range.

THE ATMOSPHERE

I once saw a globe in the storefront display window of a firm known as "World Savings." The sphere was approximately six feet tall from pole to pole. As I stood looking at the scale model, it occurred to me the distance from Denver to Pueblo, Colorado, was exactly the distance from the surface of the earth to the beginning of space. In other words, the air is approximately 100 miles from surface to surface, the distance from Denver to Pueblo.

If the scale of the model was true, on a six-foot globe, it amounted to about 3/8ths of an inch.

Science has ascertained that one-half of the air above the surface of the Earth exists below an altitude of 3.4 miles, or 18,000 feet. This means that the other half of the air is approximately 510,000 feet in height, or 96.6 miles high. I'm guessing, but in scale as illustrated above using the six-foot globe, the thickness of 3.4 miles (or 18,000 feet) would be about that of a postcard.

This doesn't seem like much air; however, when a small part of that envelope becomes unstable, an incredible amount of violence can occur.

Composition and Characteristics of the Atmosphere

The air around us is a mixture of gases composed of 79 percent nitrogen, 19 percent oxygen, and 2 percent mixed gases such as water vapor, and carbon dioxide. The air maintains this percentage composition up to the 100 mile edge.

Imagine a column of air one square inch at the bottom and extending upward to 100 miles. This column would weigh 14.7 pounds at sea level. This figures out to be .075 pounds per cubic foot. Another comparison would be that of water for the same volume. Water weighs 62 pounds per cubic foot; however, they are both fluids.

Air is a colorless, odorless, tasteless gas that contains 6.02×10^{23} molecules, under standard conditions, in a standard volume of 22.4 liters. The standard temperature is 59° F (or 15° C), and the standard pressure is 1013.2 millibars, or 29.92" of mercury at sea level. As we go higher in altitude, the air temperature drops as does the pressure. The standard temperature drop is 3 1/2 degrees per thousand feet under normal circumstances, or 5 1/2 degrees per thousand feet if forced aloft by energy within the environment.

Look at pressure by this comparison; Back in the '50s and '60s, they had a crazy fad of seeing how many people could be stuffed into a phone booth! They did it by stacking one guy upon another. Imagine the pressure on the guy at the bottom. By comparison, air is like the guys stacked in the phone booth; i.e., the guy on the bottom gets an enormous amount of weight placed on him, while the guy on top has only his own weight. Air is thick and heavy at sea level, and the pressure is great. At 18,000 feet, the pressure has dropped to approximately one-half that of sea level; therefore, the higher you go, the less the pressure.

Barometers

Pressure is measured by devices called *barometers*. There are two types. First, we have the *Torricelli* barometer. This type of pressure instrument was developed by the scientist Evangelista Torricelli. Torricelli used a long glass tube, one end of which was sealed, and the tube was filled with the element mercury. When the tube was placed upright, and the mercury allowed to drain into a bowl of mercury, a partial vacuum formed inside the tube, keeping the column from draining out. The weight of the air pushing down on the bowl of mercury also supported the column. On a standard day, this column of mercury, at sea level, was found to be 29.92" tall. That is where we get the "29.92" standard for the world, at 59° F.

The second type of barometer is called an *aneroid* and functions much like putting a toy balloon in a partial vacuum and observing the results. As the pressure drops, such as in a bell jar where the air can be pumped out using a vacuum pump, the toy balloon expands. When levers and gears are hooked up to the expanding "balloon," or bellows, specific changes in air pressure can be observed. Altimeters found on conventional aircraft use the aneroid principle. A small metallic wafer, calibrated for precise expansion, is used instead of a rubber balloon or bellows (Fig. 7-1).

You can't go over the composition of the atmosphere without a look at the presence of water.

Regardless of how dry the air may seem to be, there is always some water vapor present. The Earth's surface is about 72 percent water and through constant evaporation, the water moves into the air above. Water may exist as a vapor and only become visible when condensation occurs. Water can exist as a liquid or as a solid in the form of ice, snow, frost, hail, and so on.

Water is evaporated into the atmosphere by rivers, lakes, and of course the oceans. Warm air can hold more water than cool air and this can be compared to a clothes dryer. Warm air above a river, lake, or ocean acts like a "suction" assisting the process of evaporation. During evaporation, heat is used to convert water in its vapor state, and you can see that this evaporation would have a cooling effect on the environment simply because the heat energy required for this conversion comes from the environment.

When condensation occurs, heat energy is released to the environment; this in turn has a warming effect. When clouds are formed, a tremendous amount of latent energy is released to the environment and can, if conditions become extremely unstable, cause violence in the atmosphere.

The presence of water in the atmosphere is called *humidity*. The amount of water vapor in the air compared to how much water vapor the air can hold at the same temperature is known as the *relative humidity*. When the air is holding all of the water it can at a given temperature, this is called *saturation*. Whenever some atmospheric heat loss or cooling occurs, water may start coming out of the air and condensing on dust particles, thus forming cloud droplets, or precipitation.

Water—in the form of a fog, especially—is dangerous to a pilot flying only by visual methods. Unless you are a trained instrument pilot, you should avoid clouds and fog conditions. As you can see above, the presence of water vapor in the environ-

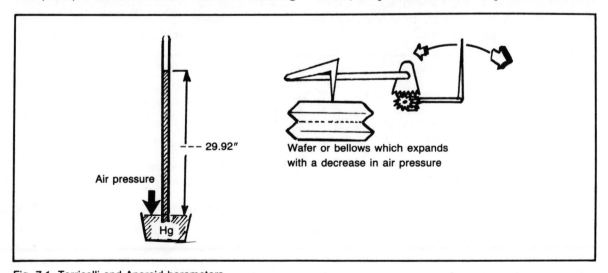

Air pressure

--- 29.92"

Hg

Wafer or bellows which expands
with a decrease in air pressure

Fig. 7-1. Torricelli and Aneroid barometers.

ment can bring about changes that may become unstable and dangerous in a very short time period.

Circulation of the Atmosphere

The sun provides the energy needed to keep the air in constant movement. The equator receives more heat per unit in a given time, and as a result, the air is constantly rising because it is lighter and more buoyant.

At the poles, the air receives less energy per unit area in a unit of time, and tends to become more dense compared to the air at the equator. A flow pattern develops toward the equator and, conversely, the air at the equator will rise to a higher altitude, flatten out, and migrate toward the poles.

If the Earth were standing still, a straight flow pattern would exist and it would be relatively simple. However, the rotation of the earth complicates this pattern and we get what is known as a *three cell circulation*. It is for this reason that the greatest movement of winds in the United States is from west to east, called the *Prevailing Westerlies.*

When the air mass starts to "pulse" due to changes in energy from the polar regions to the equator, the mass starts to move southward. The rotating Earth tends to pull this air mass to the east; thus, when you look at a TV weather map, most of the air mass movements are from northwest to southeast across the country.

If an air mass is generated in the polar regions and moves across the land surfaces, we call this source region *polar continental*. If the air mass is formed over the ocean and moves inland, it is called *maritime*. If the source region is polar and over the ocean, it would be called *polar maritime*. If the source region is over the tropical ocean, naturally it would be called *tropical maritime* (Fig. 7-2).

FRONTS AND FRONTAL CHARACTERISTICS

If the leading edge of an air mass is of different temperature characteristics than the air it is overtaking, we speak of this as a *front*. Thus a *cold front* (Fig. 7-3) is the leading edge of a mass of air that is colder than the air overtaken. Conversely, if the moving air mass is warmer than the air ahead, the leading edge would be called a *warm front* (Fig. 7-4).

The frontal profiles as indicated by their symbols (Fig. 7-5) look innocent enough; however, each front has weather that should be carefully considered by the ultralight pilot. Each front will be broken down and the characteristics pointed out that are potentially significant to the ultralight pilot:

Cold Front:

1. Wind shift.
2. Turbulence.
3. Temperature drop.

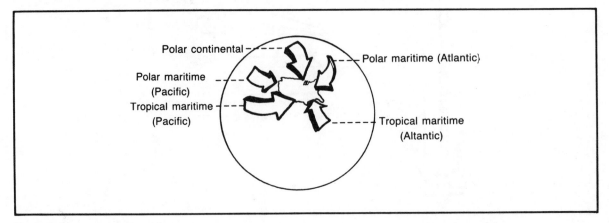

Fig. 7-2. Air mass source regions.

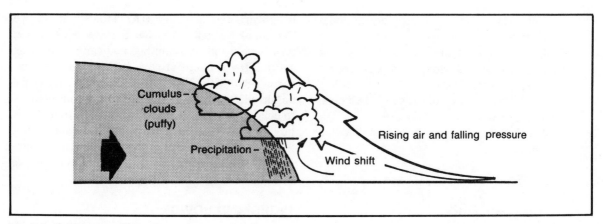

Fig. 7-3. Cold front profile.

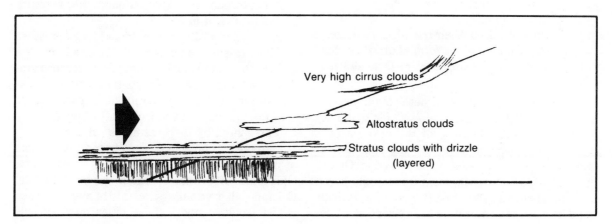

Fig. 7-4. Typical warm front profile.

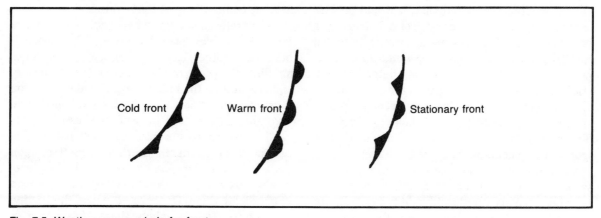

Fig. 7-5. Weather map symbols for fronts.

4. Cumulus clouds and possibly thunderstorms.
5. Unstable conditions.
6. Pressure drop ahead of, and pressure rise after passage.
7. Visibility poor as front passes, then clearing afterward.
8. Precipitation in the form of rain, snow, or hail.

Warm Front:

1. Temperature rise.
2. Stable atmosphere.
3. Poor visibility.
4. Stratus clouds.
5. Pressure drop, then rise after passage.
6. Precipitation in the form of drizzle or fog.
7. Winds may occur but very little shifting.

You can see that some of these conditions can affect your flight. If the visibility, for instance, drops to minimum because of the passage of a warm front, you might have difficulty upon arrival home if the airport happens to be socked in. On the other hand, a fast-moving cold front might come into the area so quickly that it would be difficult to make it back to home base before conditions deteriorated. Fronts can, in a very short time, turn a beautiful flying day into a pilot's nightmare!

From a practical standpoint, it would be wise to pick up a barometer and watch closely for trends. In the above statement of characteristics, note that *both* fronts had a pressure drop *in advance*. If the pressure starts falling the evening before a flight, you can almost bet on a change for the worse.

Another word of advice: Watch the local television weather reports the night before you fly. These reports will give valuable information on frontal movements in your area.

If you suspect some weather changes, and you want to be sure, or if you are planning a cross country flight, contact your local Flight Service Station for a pilot weather briefing. Look in the pages that list government agencies, (DOT) for Flight Service Station or National Weather Service. Most states now have a toll-free number you can call for this service. If you happen to live in Colorado, the number is 1-800-332-1854. Tell the FSS briefer you are an ultralight pilot and you are going from point A to point B (and returning), and the flight times. Ask him for a pilot's weather briefing and what would be his *advice* for a flight in the area you have specified. *This is not only good for you, it helps the whole ultralight aviation movement.*

HIGHS AND LOWS

Air circulates clockwise around a high pressure center and counterclockwise around a low pressure center as shown in Fig. 7-6.

Normally, air flows from areas of high pressure to low pressure. The steeper the gradient, the greater the wind velocity. A shallow pressure gradient will have light winds. As the air flows clockwise around a high, the rotation of the earth causes it to flow parallel to the isobars. In Fig. 7-7, this is represented by the "resultant" arrow.

An *isobar* represents a line of connecting points of near equal pressure. If Kansas City, Wichita, Oklahoma City, Amarillo, Raton (NM) and Pueblo, Colorado, all have a pressure of 1014 millibars, then a line would connect these cities on a surface weather map.

An *isotherm,* on the other hand, is a line connecting points of equal temperature.

Generally speaking, flying conditions are more favorable in high pressure areas. Highs usually bring fair weather, less turbulence, and more dense air. Since the winds rotate clockwise (northern hemisphere) around the high pressure center, flight on a cross-country north of the high will give you favorable tailwinds, *if you're headed east.*

Friction can be a problem in air circulation. The terrain "friction" of the Earth has an effect upon the movement of air, and will cause the low level winds to blow at an angle across the isobars, instead of parallel to them. Over water, where the friction is low, the effect will only be slight. However, over

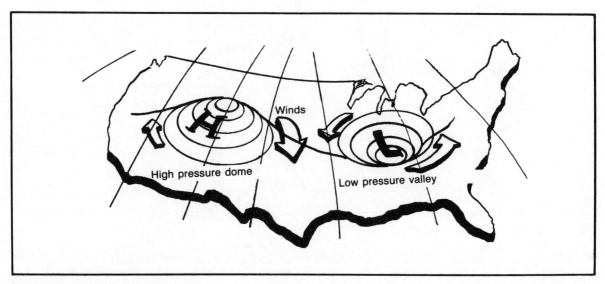

Fig. 7-6. High and low pressure areas.

the land, especially rough terrain, the variance may be as much as 50 degrees. For the ultralight pilot, this is especially important when planning a flight of extended distance. In Fig. 7-8, a modification has been made to the illustration. The winds are no longer moving at right angles to the isobars; they have veered off course due to low-altitude friction.

LOCAL SYSTEMS

During the day, the land heats up quicker than

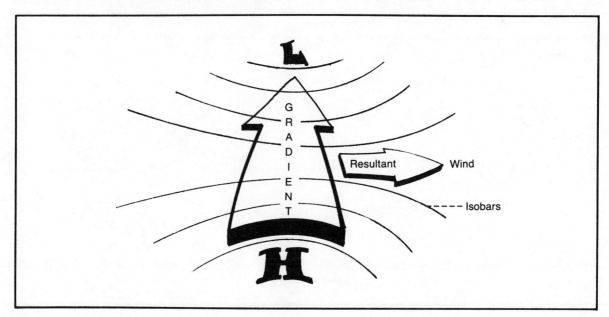

Fig. 7-7. Pressure gradient from high to low pressure areas.

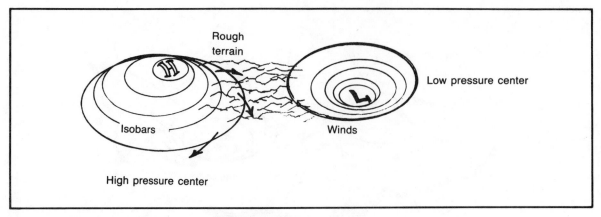

Fig. 7-8. The effect of ground friction on wind direction.

the water. The air over the heated land rises and a flow pattern of air from water to land develops (Fig. 7-9). The air rises to an altitude where it cools and replaces the sinking air over the water. This continues until evening, when the land cools and the water starts giving up some of its heat energy acquired throughout the day. The reverse movement occurs and the air will blow from the land to the water during the evening hours until equilibrium is established (Fig. 7-10).

In Fig. 7-11, you can readily see that during the daytime hours, the mountains are heated by the sun. This means that the open face of the valley gets a greater amount of radiation and in turn heats the air more than the surrounding terrain. This causes a flow outward from the center of the valley to the ridges along the edge. During the evening, the opposite occurs, since the sides radiate their energy rapidly and the cool dense air moves in to fill the void (Fig. 7-12). Due to acceleration

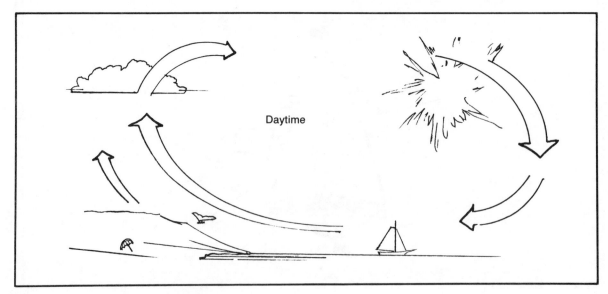

Fig. 7-9. Daytime sea breeze circulation.

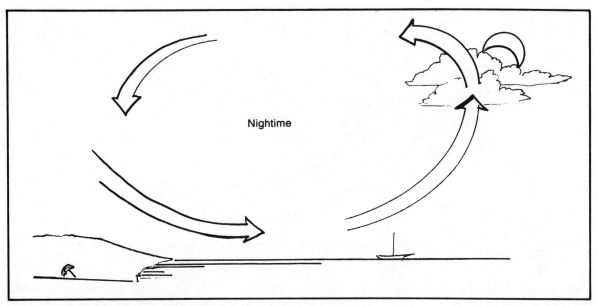

Fig. 7-10. Nighttime land breeze circulation.

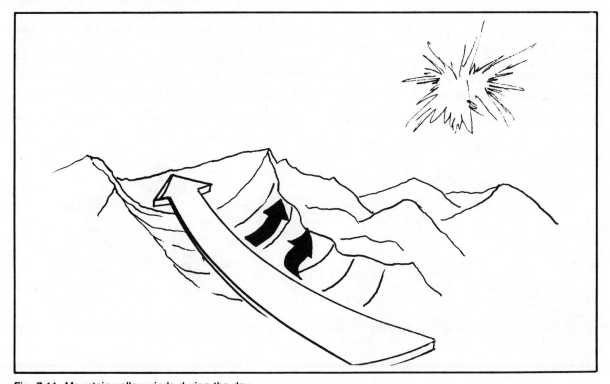

Fig. 7-11. Mountain valley winds during the day.

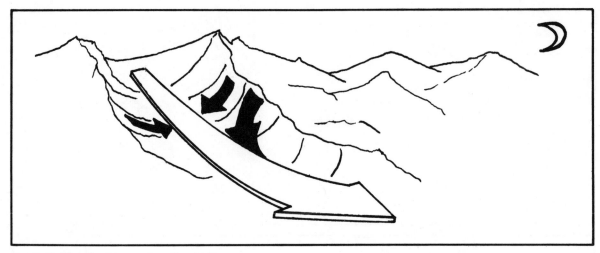

Fig. 7-12. Nighttime mountain valley winds.

energies, the night valley winds are stronger than the daytime valley winds.

Circulation Due to Convection

When the sun comes up, the Earth starts getting radiation energy. The air in the environment begins to move upward. The vertical movement depends in large part on the terrain. In Fig. 7-13, various elements in the terrain cause the air to move.

The plowed field will heat up and the air above will begin to rise; however, the air above the plowed field will not rise with the intensity of the air above a dry open area. The air above the wooded area will rise very little and the same holds true for the air over the pond.

You can see that flight over this terrain may be "bumpy" if the air is rising at different rates. Flight—especially in an ultralight—may be uncom-

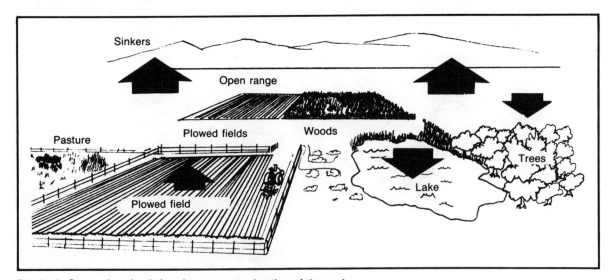

Fig. 7-13. Convective circulation due to uneven heating of the surface.

108

fortable during the midday hours when the air rises with a considerable amount of energy. A rising column of air is called a *thermal,* or more commonly known as an *updraft.* If the air is sinking at a rapid rate, the term would be *downdraft.* You will never find a "pocket" in the air, any more than you will find a pocket in water! Pilot slang usually refers to thermals as updrafts and sinkers.

One way to look at this situation is this: Think of the terrain out in front of you as it would appear through the light meter of a camera. When you see the meter rise, you can bet that you will encounter an updraft. When the meter falls, you'll get either nothing or a downdraft. In this way, the terrain will often tell you what to expect when flying over it. As the sun gets up to midday, the intensity of light and thermalling action increases. When the "light meter" in your eyes is constant, such as the day after a big snow, the air will most likely be also uniform and stable.

Circulation around Mountainous Terrain

In an FAA weather seminar, I once heard the speaker refer to air as a "fluid acting like water" when it encounters mountainous terrain. When you look at air, as it rises over, around, and through mountains, it tumbles, swirls, and becomes turbulent, much like the "white water" found in many fast-moving rivers. If the westerlies pick up a lot of energy and velocity, they can create a condition over the mountains that is treacherous. This is called a *mountain wave* (Fig. 7-14).

It should be noted that severe to extreme turbulence can be found in the above conditions. If the lens (ACSL) clouds have formed, you can be reasonably assured that turbulence will exist for miles out into the high plains. For the ultralight pilot, this constitutes a hazard to flight, even far away from the mountains.

WIND

Wind is air in motion. We have so far discussed several areas of circulation and have touched upon wind in that regard. Turbulence will usually occur when the wind is somewhere above 12 to 15 knots. Thermals are basically vertical winds and due to the uneven heating involved, may give you vertical gusts at velocities equal to or exceeding horizontal winds. One way you can spot thermalling is the presence of puffy cumulus clouds in the environment. Just remember, the clouds are the signposts of the sky, and if they puff upward, some energy source has to be involved. You can expect turbulence when a cloud is approaching your flight area. The air that is pumping the thermal may be coming from several directions and will create a gust

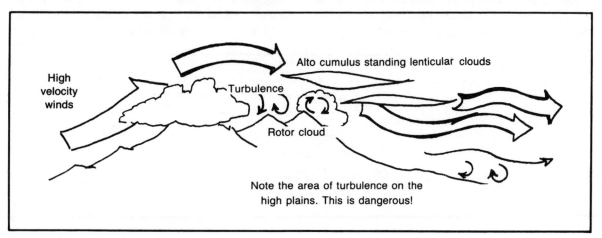

Fig. 7-14. Mountain wave conditions.

condition immediately around the thermal. Thermals on the uprising side of a hill will cause an uphill gust while thermals on the downhill side may have the opposite effect.

As a reminder, remember these points: (1) Wind blows from areas of high pressure to areas of low pressure. (2) The greater the pressure differential between the high and the low, the stronger the winds. (3) Winds blow clockwise around a high pressure area and counterclockwise around a low pressure area. When you are at home watching the local weather forecaster on TV, check out the presence of high or low pressure centers in your area. Then tie in what was given above. If a low, for instance, is south of you, you can expect winds from the east to north during the presence of the low (Fig. 7-15).

If your flight is to be in the vicinity of the low, you can predict where the winds will be from. If the terrain northeast of you is rough, you may very well have turbulence. If the terrain is smooth, flight conditions may be acceptable. If the pressure gradient is "steep" near the area where you will be flying, you can expect strong wind conditions.

Wind energy is found to be proportional to the square of its velocity. This means the force of the wind increases much faster than the wind. A 10-knot wind is *four* times more powerful than a 5-knot wind! It should be remembered that the force of a wind goes up tremendously even when the velocity increases a small amount.

Turbulence Due to Obstructions

Buildings, trees, and uneven terrain all constitute a hazard to the ultralight pilot when the wind is blowing. This is called *mechanical turbulence*. This kind of turbulence is especially hazardous during the landing and takeoff phases of flight. This type of turbulence also applies to hills and natural obstacles such as bluffs, buttes, and ridges. As the air moves upward over the obstacle, it is relatively smooth; however, once it passes the obstacle, it swirls and eddies much like water. Caution should be used when flying in wind conditions where mechanical turbulence may present a problem (Fig. 7-16).

Wind Shear

Whenever sharp changes occur in wind direction, a condition known as *wind shear* may be present. There is a zone between the wind changes that is usually rotating in all directions. This zone creates a turbulent flying condition for the ultralight. Wind shear will often exist around a temperature inversion and wind shear can be especially hazardous when in the landing or takeoff phase of your flight. An example of this would be a complete change of direction of the wind upon landing. If you were coming in with a slight headwind and your approach speed was just above stall, then the wind suddenly changed to a tailwind, you might find yourself below the speed necessary to maintain flight and the aircraft would lose altitude and cause

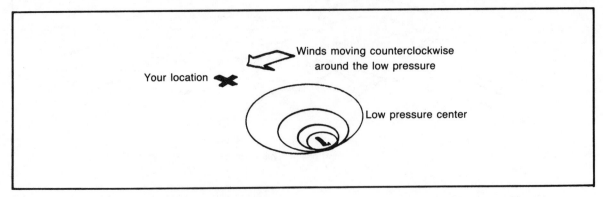

Fig. 7-15. Predictability of winds near pressure centers.

Fig. 7-16. Mechanical turbulence resulting from obstructions.

you to land short of the runway. Full power should be applied if you encounter this condition.

Turbulence from Other Aircraft

As explained earlier, wake turbulence can be a problem to all aircraft, especially if you happen to encounter it behind large transports. However, for the ultralight and its low wing loading, wake turbulence can exist even behind the light conventional aircraft such as Cessnas, Piper, and others.

Flying in the vicinity of aircraft that have already passed can create a surprise you won't be counting on. I was once told that the vortex behind a 747 in a landing configuration is enough to invert a twin Cessna *33 miles behind* the transport. True or not, it certainly makes one wonder about the hazard when you are flying anywhere within a range of 10 miles of a major airport. A good rule of thumb is to avoid the large airports and give yourself at least 10 miles of space between approach corridors for the major runways.

FOG

Fog is essentially a stratus cloud near the ground, i.e., within 50 feet of the surface. Fog consists of water drops suspended in the air. *Haze,* on the other hand, is made up of ultrafine dust and salt particles suspended in the air. The difference is the

feel; fog is damp due to the moisture.

The main hazard with fog is the restriction to visibility. If fog happens while you are flying, it may completely eliminate your landing visibility.

The conditions that generate fog are easy to remember. First, there must be a *high humidity* in order to get the condensation. The point where the air will condense is called the *dewpoint.* When the temperature and dewpoint are within 4°, a fog may be forming. The most frequently encountered temperature for the start of fog is 2° spread between the temperature and the dewpoint. Wind—generally light—is necessary for a mixing action. Finally, there has to be *condensation nuclei,* such as particles of salt, dust, or smoke, suspended in the atmosphere. The nuclei give the moisture a point of attachment.

DENSITY ALTITUDE

Density altitude is pressure altitude corrected for non-standard temperature.

One of the reasons I have included this in your ground school training is obvious to those of us who live in the high plains and mountainous areas. Density altitude is a "pilot killer," and the more you know about its effects, the better off you will be.

The 15°N. Latitude (std) temperature, at sea level, is 59°F. As the air rises, it cools by a standard lapse rate of 3 1/2° per thousand feet. The *standard* temperature for any elevation higher than sea level is *lower* than 59°F. Denver, for example, has a standard temperature of 41.5°F. Here are the standard temperatures for the elevations, in thousand foot increments, up to 8000 feet.

Sea Level	59.0°F
1000 feet	55.5°F
2000 feet	52.0°F
3000 feet	48.5°F
4000 feet	45.0°F
5000 feet	41.5°F
6000 feet	38.0°F
7000 feet	34.5°F
8000 feet	31.0°F

Going back to our definition, density altitude is pressure altitude corrected for non-standard temperature. If the temperature at 5000 feet is 41.5° F, the airplane will have predictable performance expectations. It will have a given engine output, a predictable climb performance, etc. Let conditions change, such as a higher temperature and a higher humidity, and the performance of the aircraft will change, usually decreasing. An example of what happens is this: If the temperature in Denver is 80°F, the airplane will no longer perform like it is at 5000 feet; rather it will perform like it would at approximately 7800 feet. Now you know why on muggy, hot summer days, your airplane will hardly climb out of its shadow.

Three factors enter the picture: high altitude, high temperature, and high humidity. Just remember these words and take measures of caution and correction when they occur simultaneously: "High, hot, and humid."

THUNDERSTORMS

One of nature's most violent forms of weather is the thunderstorm. The thunderstorm has all of the elements of a pilot's nightmare; it goes without saying they should be avoided.

Thunderstorms are the result of instability in the atmosphere. There has to be some force that causes the air to be lifted, and there has to be relatively high moisture content within the atmosphere. Various factors may be involved in the "lifting" action: (1) orographic forces such as terrain; (2) frontal lifting such as would be found at the leading edge of a cold front; (3) convection such as you might find on a hot summer afternoon over the plains. A thunderstorm usually occurs because of a *convective cell,* or an isolated cell of energies. They vary from one to five miles in diameter. It should be noted that the life cycle of an average thunderstorm is from one-half to two hours.

The initial stage of a thunderstorm consists of a buildup of the cumulus cloud. Not all cumulous clouds have the potential to become a thunderstorm, but some develop energies that become progressively more violent. These energies cause vertical currents of air that may reach 5000 feet per minute and cause even greater instability within the storm. Eventually, condensation occurs within the cell and rain is formed.

As the rain begins to fall, the air within is dragged toward the surface. The downward movement of air, or *downdraft,* begins to accelerate, often reaching velocities of 2500 feet per minute. The up and down drafts cause wind shear to occur and gusting results in and near the cell. These gusts are severe enough to cause structure failure in conventional aircraft.

Finally energies within the storm dissipate and the cell turns into a downdraft flow pattern.

One thing the ultralight pilot should know is the existence of "tornado" tubes near the edge of the cell. These tubes are invisible and can literally suck an aircraft up into the cloud. Hail can also be thrown out of the top of the cloud and it can throw these ice balls several miles away from the storm. Always give the thunderstorm a minimum of five miles horizontal leeway. The weather near a thunderstorm is generally quite unstable and flight in an ultralight is not recommended under these conditions.

PREDICTING WEATHER

After years of watching TV weather, you can predict some local weather conditions with a certain degree of accuracy by observing their reports. TV weather persons are, for the most part, well-trained individuals. With new technologies, the National Weather Service is claiming 80 percent accuracy oftentimes. TV meteorologists get their background information from the National Weather Service. Sometimes, unfortunately, what a local TV station says may not apply to *your* locale. Using the weather information previously presented in this chapter, and a few "tried and true" methods of forecasting, you might be able to get an idea of what's going on in the environment.

The old nautical expression, "Red sky at night, sailor's delight," is quite good for predicting what is in store for the next morning's flight. The reason for the expression is this: Most of our weather, as stated earlier, comes from the west. Therefore, at sundown, if the sky is totally red, no clouds are present or expected, and quite likely a good clear morning will follow. If the sky is red in the morning ("sailor take warning"), it means clouds to the east are forming and bending the light into the red part of the spectrum, giving an indication of possible rain showers forthcoming.

Another good indicator is a clear, starry night. Generally, if it is clear at night, your morning flight will be a good one. If dew or frost is present in the morning, it is a good sign, since the absence of clouds during the night allowed the heavy dew or frost formation.

High-flying birds are a good sign. This means there is high pressure in the region and if birds are not flying at all, there is possibly low pressure around the area. Birds have a sense for pressure and has a tendency to sink in low pressure.

THE ULTRALIGHT CONNECTION

It was once said that flying is 999.9 hours of boredom and about .1 of an hour of sheer terror. Fact or fiction, you can bet that the one-tenth of an hour of terror is most likely weather-related. For the ultralight pilot, some of the most terrifying moments will be spent in the cockpit getting kicked around by turbulent, unstable air.

I want to leave you with the following in hopes that it will bring the ultralight into perspective with the environment. In this way, I hope to make the all-important "ultralight connection!"

If you examine the wing area of an average ultralight, you will find that it is very close to that of the Cessna 152 trainer. The Cessna has a wing span of just over 33 feet and a chord of slightly less than 5 feet. A Quicksilver MX has a wing span of 32 feet and a chord of 5 feet. This gives a wing area of 160 square feet for both aircraft. Now you have to take a look at the weight difference. The weight of a loaded C152 is right at 1600 pounds; the Quicksilver with pilot and fuel should come in around 400 pounds. Enter another factor called *wing loading*. Wing loading is found by dividing the weight by the square footage, or area, of the wing. The wing loading of the Cessna is 10 pounds per square foot while the Quicksilver is 2.5 pounds per square foot. You can immediately see how, if the wing area is the same, what is just a little bump to a Cessna can turn out to be a riot in an ultralight. I am referring, of course, to *turbulence*.

A Cessna might experience a bit of uncomfortable "chop" during some buckaroo weather while the ultralight will be all over the sky. In comparison, consider a bumpy road in a car and then going over the same road on a bicycle. When the air is dead calm and perfectly stable, the flight in an ultralight can be a sensation; however, if the movements of the air are somewhat on the rough side you may very well have your one-tenth of an hour of sheer terror!

Take weather seriously and get weather briefings from the NWS or the Flight Service Station. In the first few hours of flight, fly only in those calm hours of the day when you can get to know your aircraft. Later, when you have some experience, you can tackle the turbulence. Enjoy your flying and spend the initial time perfecting the techniques of mastering the craft. Once you know your aircraft, the good habits you learned come naturally and then you can cope with the environment.

Glossary

Glossary

absolute altitude—The altitude of an aircraft above the terrain.

absolute ceiling—The maximum altitude an aircraft can attain and still hold straight and level flight.

acceleration—The rate of velocity increase.

aerobatic—Stunt flying or the act of doing stunts with an aircraft.

aerodrome—An airport.

aerodynamic—The forces acting upon a body moving through the air.

aileron—A control surface that produces a rolling moment around the longitudinal axis of the aircraft.

aileron flutter—A vibration occurring in some ailerons due to instability in the control surface.

aileron roll—A maneuver in which the aircraft rotates around the longitudinal axis and the performance of which is entirely done by operation of the ailerons.

aileron yaw—The yaw produced by the induced drag of the high wing aileron in a banked turn.

airfoil—A surface that produces a dynamic change in the air as it passes over that surface.

airframe—The structural components of any aircraft. In the ultralight, this would include tubes, gear, spars, engine mounts, etc.

airplane—The FAA defines this as "an engine-driven fixed-wing aircraft heavier than air that is supported in flight by dynamic reaction of the air against its wings."

airport—"An area of land or water that is used or intended to be used for the landing and take-off of aircraft, and includes its buildings and facilities, if any." (FAR, Part 1)

Airport Traffic Area—"Means, unless otherwise specified in Part 93, that airspace within a horizontal radius of 5 statute miles from the geographical center of any airport at which a control tower is operating, extending from the surface up to, but not including, an altitude of 3,000 feet above the elevation of the airport." (FAA)

airship—An engine-driven lighter-than-air aircraft

that can be steered.

airspeed—The speed of the aircraft through the air mass.

airspeed indicator—An instrument that shows the speed of the aircraft through the air mass.

airstream—The relative airflow around the aircraft or the propeller.

airstrip—A grass, earth, or paved surface that is used for takeoff and landing of aircraft.

air traffic—The flow of air traffic within a given air space, such as an airport or airway.

Air Traffic Control—"A service operated by appropriate authority to promote the safe, orderly, and expeditious flow of air traffic." (FAA)

airway—A designated "highway" in the sky designated for air traffic.

airworthy—The condition of being safe for flight.

altimeter—A pressure instrument used for indication of altitude. The altimeter is usually set to register above sea level.

altitude—The elevation of the aircraft above a plane of reference.

angle of attack—The angle between the chordline of the wing and the relative wind.

angle of incidence—The "built-in" angle of an aircraft component.

appliance—"Any instrument, mechanism, equipment, part, apparatus, appurtenance, or accessory, including communications equipment, that is used or intended to be used in operating or controlling an aircraft in flight, is installed in or attached to the aircraft, and is not part of an airframe, engine, or propeller." (FAA)

approved—" . . . approved by the Administrator." (FAA)

attitude—The presented aspect of an aircraft at any given moment.

axis—The supposed or theoretical line extending through the center of gravity. An aircraft has three axes (plural) about which it rotates: longitudinal, lateral, and vertical.

azimuth—An angular bearing measured clockwise from north or zero degrees on a 360 degree circle.

bank—To roll the aircraft around the longitudinal axis of the aircraft in flight.

best angle of climb—An airspeed that gives the greatest gain in altitude in a given distance.

best rate of climb—The airspeed that gives the greatest gain altitude in a given amount of time.

brake horsepower—"The power delivered at the propeller shaft of an aircraft engine." (FAA)

buffet—A drumming or beating effect usually associated with a burbling of the air on top of the wing during a stall.

burble—The turbulence created when the boundary layer of air on the upper side of the wing separates from the airfoil.

calibrated airspeed—"Indicated airspeed of an aircraft, corrected for position and instrument error. Calibrated airspeed is equal to true airspeed in a standard atmosphere at sea level." (FAA)

category—"As used with respect to the certification of aircraft, means a grouping of aircraft based upon intended use or operating limitations. Examples include: transport; normal; utility; aerobatic; limited; restricted; and provisional." (FAA)

ceiling—"The height above the Earth's surface of the lowest layer of clouds or obscuring phenomena that is reported as 'broken', 'overcase', or 'obscuration', and not classified as 'thin' or 'partial'." (FAA)

center of gravity—All of the force of gravity goes through this point. If an aircraft were hanging straight and level from a cable attached to the ceiling of a hangar, the point where the three axes intersected on the cable would be the center of gravity. This is often spoken of as the CG.

center of gravity range—The distance between the most forward and most aft center-of-gravity limits.

center of lift—The average of all the centers of pressure on a lifting body such as an airfoil.

center of pressure—The point along the airfoil's chord in which you will find all the resultant forces acting on that airfoil.

center of thrust—A line about which the forces of thrust are balanced.

check list—A list of items to be covered in a procedure such as preflight and pretakeoff.

checkpoint—A reference point used for checking the position of an aircraft in flight.

chinook—A warm, dry wind blowing down the eastern slopes of a mountain, usually referred to the Rocky Mountain eastern slopes blowing toward the high plains.

chord—An assumed line between the leading and trailing edges of an airfoil.

climb—The ascension of an aircraft under some form of power.

cloud—A visible gathering of water particles in the atmosphere.

cockpit—The space for the pilot.

controllability—"The capability of an airplane to respond to the pilot's control, especially with regard to flight path and attitude. It is the quality of the airplane's response to the pilot's control application when maneuvering the airplane, regardless of its stability characteristics." (FAA)

controls—The devices used in operation of the aircraft.

control stick—A stick that activates the controls, sometimes called a *joystick*.

course—The direction toward the destination as charted, described in degrees of deviation from north. True course is measured from true north and magnetic course is measured from magnetic north.

crab angle—The wind or drift correction angle.

critical angle of attack—The angle of attack which an airplane stalls or that angle where the boundary layer of air separates from the upper surface of the wing.

crosswind—A wind blowing across the aircraft line of flight.

cruise speed—A level-flight speed that is the result of a specific power setting as recommended by the aircraft manufacturer for cruise flight.

cumulonimbus—A thunderstorm type of cloud that is to be avoided by all types of aircraft. It is heavy and dense, with considerable vertical development, often with towers or a massive plume. Under this cloud is usually found lightning, hail, rain, wind shear, possible tornadoes, and violent wind shift conditions.

dead reckoning navigation—A form of navigation that considers the wind correction, the course, the compass and magnetic variations, time and the speed of the craft.

deadstick landing—A landing made without power. It is essentially a gliding approach.

density—The mass per unit volume or as spoken in terms of the air; this would be the molecules per unit volume.

deviation—A compass error caused by disturbances within the aircraft.

dewpoint—The temperature to which air must be cooled to condense.

dihedral—The angle formed between the root of the wing and the wing tip.

downdraft—A column of air that moves downward.

downwind—In a direction *with* the wind.

downwind landing—A landing made with the wind to the pilot's back.

downwind leg—The leg in the traffic pattern of an airport that is opposite the direction of the landing runway.

downwind turn—A turn made away from the wind.

drag—The force that opposes the aircraft's forward movement.

drift—Deflection of the aircraft from its intended course.

dual ignition—An ignition system in which the cylinders of an airplane's engine are fired by separate ignition systems.

elevator—The control surface attached to the horizontal stabilizer used to cause a pitch change around the lateral axis.

empennage—The rear control surfaces including

the elevator, stabilizers, and rudder.

ETA—Estimated time of arrival.

ETE—Estimated time enroute.

ETD—Estimated time of departure.

fairing—A structure that usually surrounds an area or component and is expressly designed to minimize drag.

fin—Another name for the vertical stabilizer.

flap—A control that works, (usually) to increase the camber of the inboard portion of the wing. This surface increases lift and acts as a mechanism of increasing drag.

flare—A maneuver executed by increasing the angle of attack just before the point of touchdown.

flight line—A tiedown area for aircraft and the areas surrounding the hangars and service areas. This does not include the runways or taxiways.

flight path—The line of flight an aircraft takes through the air.

flight plan—Information relating to the intended flight that is written out and usually made available to some outside person or agency.

fog—A cloud at or near the surface of the Earth, consisting of visible moisture.

fore—Toward the front of the vehicle.

form drag—Drag caused by the shape of an object.

fuel-air ratio—The ratio of the air to the fuel as it is entering the combustion chamber of the aircraft engine.

fuselage—The main "body" of the aircraft.

G—The pull of the Earth upon a unit mass.

general aviation—That segment of aviation which includes all aircraft other than military or commercial airlines. Ultralights are considered a part of general aviation.

glide—Flight maintained only by the loss of altitude.

glide angle—The angle between the glide path and the horizon.

glide path—The forward line of the aircraft as it descends in a glide.

glide ratio—The ratio of the forward distance traveled to the loss in altitude in the same time frame.

glider—An aircraft that is heavier than air and does not depend upon a powerplant to sustain flight.

ground effect—A cushion or influence that is caused by a rebounding of air from the surface to a low-flying aircraft. The ground effect usually becomes apparent when an aircraft is within about the distance of its own wingspan above the surface.

ground roll—The landing rollout.

ground speed—The speed of the aircraft across the ground over which it flies.

ground visibility—The horizontal visibility near the surface of the earth as reported by an observer (accredited).

gyroscope—A device that has a rotor wheel mounted so it is free to rotate in two axes perpendicular to itself and to each other.

haze—Fine dust particles scattered throughout the atmosphere. Haze decreases horizontal visibility.

heading—Course corrections made for wind. Also the direction in which the nose of the aircraft points during a flight.

high wing—An aircraft wing mounted near the top of the fuselage.

horizon—The line where the Earth and sky meet.

horsepower—A unit of measuring the output of an engine. It is the power required to raise 550 pounds through a distance of one foot in a time of one second.

humidity—The water vapor content in the air.

hypoxia—A deficiency of oxygen.

induced drag—Drag produced when an airfoil is lifting.

instability—A condition of being unstable. This is often referred to in the study of the atmosphere when considerable vertical lifting is present.

interference drag—Drag caused by the interaction of components such as wings to fuselage and stabilizer to fin, etc.

kinesthesia—A sense that will detect motion without references to hearing or vision.

knot—A measure of velocity per hour which is 6076 feet (in approximate value).

landing—The act of terminating flight and bringing the airplane to rest.

landing speed—The minimum speed that a pilot can land an aircraft and still maintain control.

lateral stability—The stability of an aircraft around the longitudinal axis.

leading edge—The front edge of an airfoil.

lean—A reduction of the fuel in a fuel to air mixture.

lift—A force created by pressure differential on an airfoil induced by the dynamic reaction of air.

lift coefficient—A number that gives the relative lift for a given airfoil.

lift to drag ratio—The ratio of lift to the amount of drag of an airfoil. This is found by dividing the lift by the drag coefficient.

load—The static or dynamic forces acting upon a body.

load factor—Sum total of loads on a body, usually expressed in units known as Gs.

longitudinal axis—The axis of an aircraft that goes from nose to tail and passes through the center of gravity.

lower camber—The curvature of the airfoil on the bottom side.

maneuverability—"The quality of an airplane that permits it to be maneuvered easily and to withstand the stresses imposed by maneuvers. It is governed by the aircraft weight, inertia, size and location of flight controls, structural strength, and the powerplant. It too is an airplane design characteristic." (FAA)

maneuvering speed—The maximum speed at which the controls can be fully deflected without damage to the aircraft's structural integrity.

In conventional aircraft, it is the speed the pilot would keep the aircraft when encountering severe turbulence.

maximum gross weight—The maximum weight authorized by the manufacturer for operation under normal conditions (ultralight type aircraft).

mean sea level—The average level of the ocean, or sea, as one would use to compute barometric pressure.

measured ceiling—The height of the lowest layer of clouds that would be determined to be a ceiling, as observed by a ceilometer, or by known heights of unobscured portions of objects, other than natural landmarks within 1 1/2 miles (knots) of the airport.

millibar—A unit of pressure equal to a force of 1000 dynes per square centimeter. There are approximately 34 millibars per inch of barometric pressure.

minimum flying speed—(As used in slow flight maneuvers): The lowest speed that can be maintained in straight and level flight.

nautical mile—A unit of distance that is 6076 feet in length. This unit is 1.15 statute miles.

navaid—A device that provides point-to-point guidance information.

nose—The forward end of the aircraft.

nose dive—A steep pitch-down dive.

Notice To Airmen (NOTAM)—A notice containing information not known sufficiently in advance to publicize by other means concerning the establishment, condition or change in any component, facility service or procedure of, or hazard in the National Air Space System, the timely knowledge of which is essential to concerned personnel and flight operations.

oleo strut—A shock absorber used in some landing gear systems wherein the shock is absorbed by a hydraulic action.

orientation flight—An introductory flight to familiarize the student with the aircraft.

overcontrol—To use the control in excess of what is necessary for the intended maneuver.

overcast—In surface weather observations, it is a sky condition with clouds that exceeds .9 coverage.

overshoot—To fly beyond a point of intent.

pilotage—Navigation by reference to landmarks; point-to-point navigation using points of reference or maps, or both.

pitch—The movement of an aircraft about its lateral axis or the blade angle of the propeller.

positive Gs—A force exerted upon the pilot when pulling out of a dive. The weight of the pilot (the outside forces on the body) increases in a positive G situation.

power loading—The power-to-weight ratio. This number can be found by dividing the weight by the horsepower of the engine.

powerplant—The engine and all of the accessories, including propeller, fuel supply, electrical, etc.

preflight—To check the aircraft or system before use.

propeller—An airfoil that is operated directly by the engine and upon rotation, creates forward thrust.

prop wash—The turbulent air behind the propeller, created by the propeller.

pusher—An aircraft wherein the propeller is mounted aft of the engine and pushes the air away from it.

rate of climb—The vertical component of flight when an aircraft is climbing.

rate of descent—The vertical component of flight when an aircraft is descending.

relative wind—The direction of the airflow with respect to the aircraft, more specifically the airfoil.

rig—Making certain adjustments in an aircraft (ultralight) that will deliver specific flight characteristics.

rime ice—The opaque or milky white granular deposits of ice often found on the leading edge of airfoils that encounter icing conditions. Rime is formed by the rapid freezing of supercooled water drops as they form upon an exposed surface.

roll—Movement about the longitudinal axis.

rudder—A movable control surface attached to the vertical stabilizer (usually) and functions to yaw the aircraft around the vertical axis.

rudder pedals—A pair of pedals that operate the rudder. In the case of some ultralights, these pedals are used to operate the spoilerons and are not attached to the rudder of the aircraft.

runway—An area dedicated to the landing and taking off of aircraft.

skid—Lateral motion of the aircraft produced by centrifugal force.

slip—The motion of the aircraft in which it is moving to the inside of the turn.

slipstream—The movement of the air driven rearward by the propeller.

solo—Flight in which a pilot is the only occupant of the aircraft.

span—The distance from wingtip to wingtip.

spar—The principal longitudinal member of the wing.

spin—A prolonged stall in which the aircraft rotates about its center of gravity while descending.

spiral—A prolonged descending turn at least 360 degrees in rotation.

stability—"The inherent quality of an aircraft to correct for conditions that may disturb its equilibrium, and to return or to continue on the original flightpath."

stabilizer—The fixed airfoil attached to the fuselage that increases stability. The elevator and rudder are attached to stabilizers.

stall—The condition that occurs when the critical angle of attack has been exceeded and the airflow over the airfoil no longer provides lift by the dynamic reaction to the airfoil.

stall speed—The speed at which the aircraft will

stall. If the aircraft has gear down and flaps down, this is referred to as V_{S0}. If the gear and flaps are up, it is referred to as V_{S1}.

standard atmosphere—A hypothetical atmosphere based on climatic averages. The parameters of a standard atmosphere are 59°F (15°C), 29.92 inches of mercury, or 1013.2 millibars, and a metric pressure of 760 millimeters.

standard lapse rate—A decrease in temperature of approximately 2° Celsius, or 3 1/2°F., per 1000 feet gain altitude.

statute mile—A standard 5280 foot mile.

stratiform clouds—Clouds that display extensive horizontal development. These clouds are generally quite stable and are composed of small water droplets.

syllabus—A list of points or topics to be covered (usually an outline) given by an instructor to a student showing the ground and flight training to be covered.

tab—A small auxiliary part of the airfoil, usually part of the primary control surfaces, that serves the purpose of taking the control pressure away from the pilot's hands and feet.

tail—The aft part of the aircraft.

taildragger—An airplane that has a tailwheel instead of the more common tricycle landing gear.

tailheavy—A condition wherein the aircraft has a tendency to sink aft of the lateral axis when the flight control is released.

tailspin—An outdated term meaning the same as a spin.

tailwind—Condition when aircraft is flying in same direction as the air mass that supports it.

takeoff—The action of getting the aircraft into the air.

takeoff distance—The distance required to get the aircraft to fly.

takeoff run—Takeoff distance.

takeoff speed—The forward speed required to get the aircraft flying.

taxi—The movement of the aircraft on the ground or water by its own power.

throttle—The power control of an aircraft.

thrust—The forward force of the aircraft provided by a power unit.

torque—A twisting force.

touch-and-go landing—A landing in which the aircraft transitions from landing to another take-off without coming to a full stop.

touchdown—That part of the landing sequence when the wheels touch the runway or landing surface.

track—The flight path over the ground.

traffic pattern—The traffic flow around an airport in which the aircraft are landing, taxiing, or taking off. There are several components of a traffic pattern: upwind, crosswind, downwind, base, and final approach legs.

traffic pattern indicators—Markers associated with the runway system such as the segmented circle expressly for the purpose of controlling the direction of traffic.

trim—To adjust an aircraft so that it is properly balanced, in terms of the flight controls.

true airspeed—The actual speed of the aircraft through the air. It is the calibrated airspeed corrected for temperature and air density.

true altitude—The altitude above sea level (mean).

turbulence—The irregular motion of the atmosphere produced when air becomes unstable.

upwind—Into the wind.

useful load—The difference between the empty weight of aircraft and the recommended gross weight. This is sometimes referred to as *payload*.

visibility—The greatest horizontal distance from which unlighted prominent objects can be seen (on the ground); for weather observing purposes, visibility is categorized as (1) meteorological visibility, (2) vertical visibility, or (3) runway visual range.

VFR—Visual Flight Rules.

VOR—Very high frequency omnirange station.

vortices—Circular patterns of airflow created by

the movement of an airfoil through the atmosphere. The term *wake turbulence* is commonly used to describe these vortices.

wash—Disturbed air.

wash-in—A greater angle of incidence built into a wing to provide more pressure differential. This is a method manufacturers use to offset the effects of torque.

washout—A lesser angle of incidence built into an airfoil to decrease lift as compared to the opposite wing.

weathercock—The tendency of an aircraft on the ground to align itself to the wind.

wind correction angle—An angle necessary to compensate for drift. Also called the *crab angle* or WCA.

wind shear—The change of either wind speed or direction or both in any direction expressed as vertical or horizontal wind shear.

wing—An airfoil whose function it is to provide lift by the dynamic reaction between it and the relative wind.

wing root—That end of the wing closest to the fuselage.

wing tip—The end of the wing farthest from the fuselage.

wingspan—The distance from wingtip to wingtip.

yaw—To turn about the vertical axis.

zoom—A steep, fast climb.

Zulu Time—Greenwich universal time, or Greenwich Mean Time (GMT).

Index

Index

Other Bestsellers From TAB

☐ **GOOD TAKEOFFS AND GOOD LANDINGS—Joe Christy**

This book is a reference that thoroughly examines takeoffs and landings, and the critical transitions accompanying each, for single-engine aircraft. The author stresses that every pilot must continuously evaluate ever-changing factors of wind, air pressure, precipitation, traffic, temperature, visibility, runway length, and braking conditions. *Good Takeoffs and Good Landings* belongs on every pilot's required reading list. 192 pp., 70 illus.

Paper $14.95   **Hard $21.95**
Book No. 2487

☐ **LIGHTPLANE REFURBISHING TECHNIQUES—Joe Christy**

Discover how you can save up to 80 percent of the cost of refurbishing a lightplane using the new FAA-approved aircraft recovering, painting, and interior refurbishing materials that were introduced in the early 1980's—lightweight Dacrons with special finishes, the water-based Ceconite 7600 system, and new plastic beads which can strip old paint from aluminum alloy aircraft skins without damaging the aluminum coating. 160 pp., 160 illus.

Paper $12.95   **Hard $18.95**
Book No. 2437

☐ **AUTOMOBILE ENGINES FOR AIRPLANES—Joe Christy**

Aviation expert Joe Christy comes through again for today's cost-conscious homebuilder with an invaluable sourcebook that shows you how to convert an automobile engine for use in your homebuilt. You'll learn what critical considerations must be addressed when changing an automobile engine into a dependable, efficient aircraft powerplant. 176 pp., 87 illus.

Paper $14.95   **Book No. 2447**

☐ **FLIGHT BRIEFING FOR ULTRALIGHT PILOTS— N.H. Birch, A.E. Bramson, and Joe Christy**

Flying excitement without the high costs and stringent licensing requirements of conventional lightplanes . . . no wonder ultralights have been enjoying such growing popularity across the U.S., and worldwide! Now, *Aviators' Guild* brings you an ultralight guide that's guaranteed to make your flying time safer and more enjoyable. It even prepares you for transition to conventional airplanes. 288 pp., 129 illus.

Paper $14.95   **Book No. 2417**

*Prices subject to change without notice.

To purchase these or any other books from TAB, visit your local bookstore, return this coupon, or call toll-free 1-800-233-1128 (In PA and AK call 1-717-794-2191).

Product No.	Hard or Paper	Title	Quantity	Price

☐ Check or money order enclosed made payable to TAB BOOKS Inc.

Charge my   ☐ VISA   ☐ MasterCard   ☐ American Express

Acct. No. _____ Exp. _____

Signature _____

Please Print
Name _____

Company _____

Address _____

City _____

State _____ Zip _____

Subtotal	
Postage/Handling ($5.00 outside U.S.A. and Canada)	$2.50
In PA add 6% sales tax	
TOTAL	

Mail coupon to:

TAB BOOKS Inc.
Blue Ridge Summit
PA 17294-0840   BC